THE HOUSE THAT JACK BOUGHT

A Scotsman and his Lodgers
in the Spanish Hinterland

JACK WALDIE

Text copyright ©2019 Jack Waldie

The author has asserted his moral right under the Copyright, Designs and Patents Act, 1988, to be identified as the author of this work.

All rights reserved. No part of this publication may be reproduced, stored in a retrieval system, or transmitted, in any form or by any means, without the prior permission in writing of the publisher.

1

We bought the house on a whim. It seemed remarkably cheap at the time and my wife and I fell in love with it during a tour of the area which has become known as *la Laponia española*, or Spanish Lapland, due to it containing even fewer inhabitants per square mile than the frosty one up in Finland. It felt rather eerie driving on deserted roads and staying in places with far fewer people than their size warranted, but we enjoyed our week of peace, quiet and fresh air. In one relatively lively village we strolled out in the evening and saw the house in question.

"Look, it's for sale. It'd make a good rural lodging house like the one we're staying at." said Nicola.

"I doubt there's much demand around here. The owner looked mightily pleased to see us." I gazed at the stone house and its red roof. "It's a big old place too. It'll not be cheap."

"We'll find out tomorrow."

"Are you serious?"

"Nothing ventured, nothing gained, Jack."

"I guess not."

"You could write in peace here."

"Hmm."
"And I could try to work online."
"No harm in asking, I suppose."
"And we need a change."
"Yes, I think we do."

The following day we viewed the house, liked the dusty old place, signed a document the estate agent had knocked up, and paid a small deposit. I believe the brisk young man suspected we'd get cold feet when we returned to Glasgow and was pleased to have the five hundred in his pocket, but a month later we duly returned and the detached, two-storey, four-bedroom house became ours. It was structurally quite sound, but Nicola insisted on getting the builders in right away to reform it from top to bottom. We got two quotes – both for considerably more than what the house had cost – and chose the slightly dearer one because the builder was a local man.

"The costs mount," I murmured on signing the building contract.

"Your book's doing well."

"For now," I said, as my latest crime thriller had been received more warmly than the four I'd already written. After the third I'd packed in my teaching job, had soon begun to regret that rash decision, but had perked up lately due to the steady sales of my latest effort. I write my thrillers under a pen name and won't plug those books here. This one will be different. Flights of fancy won't be permitted and, if truth be told, aren't required.

We camped in the house for a few days, got some essential paperwork done with the estate agent's help, and made lots of plans for the future. We were both mildly excited about our new start in Spain which would commence the following spring.

That autumn, despite our new project giving us plenty to talk about, things began to go awry between Nicola and I. She was thirty-three – six years younger than me – and we'd been married for eight years. We'd been trying to have a baby for most of that time. We'd tried IVF twice to no avail and after a private consultation had discovered that my sperm didn't behave in the way it should. Since then Nicola had met someone else and in April we agreed to part.

"I guess we'll have to sell the house here and the one in Spain and reckon up," she said glumly one evening, as she felt awfully guilty about the whole business.

"If you're happy to keep this, I'll keep the house in Spain," I found myself saying, despite not having set eyes on the place for eight months, though the builder had assured me repeatedly that our bank transfers were being put to good effect. The occasional photos his son emailed us appeared to confirm this.

"Oh, but this place is worth far more," she said.

"I don't care. I don't want complications."

"I'm really sorry this has happened, Jack."

"Life goes on. I'll move next month when the house is finished."

"All right, but I'll owe you. If you need money just ask."

"But there's still a mortgage on this place."

She swatted the air. "Just a small one."

The sales of my novel had slowed and her new man was a doctor – one of those whom we'd met at the private clinic, in fact, such are life's ironies – so if my next book flopped I might need a bit of help, but I'd do my damnedest to avoid asking for handouts. She'd backed me up when I'd chosen the precarious writer's life and her substantial salary had made that possible, so I felt she'd already done enough for me.

I moved out at the end of May, taking only a suitcase and a travel bag containing my precious laptops. Nicola wished me well and promised to look after my books and other belongings. Ours was a civilised separation and although I felt disappointed and even somewhat diminished, I was determined to make the most of my new life.

2

La Laponia española is a phrase coined by a journalist, I believe, as the area's official name is *La Serranía Celtibérica*. It comprises the hilly, partly wooded area some way to the east of Madrid, stretching from the southernmost parts of Soria and Zaragoza down to Cuenca and Teruel. People have been leaving for decades, the population is ageing, schools closing, villages becoming abandoned. Few of them were ever very large and many are at over a thousand metres above sea level. This makes for harsh winters which combined with the mediocre soil leads one to wonder how they ever prospered, but they did for at least a couple of thousand years. The industrial revolution came late to Spain, but when it did – towards the end of the nineteenth century – the first wave of emigration towards Barcelona and Madrid began. Since then it hasn't stopped and they're crying out for people to cast away their urban cares and move there.

Now they would have a thirty-nine-year-old Scotsman whose sperm might not be up to propagating, but that was the last thing on my mind as I drove my car the 110 miles roughly east from Madrid. I'd taken a taxi to the town of

Torrejón de Ardoz and bought a second-hand Suzuki 4x4 that I'd enquired about by email, intending to be prepared for the snow that was said to fall every winter. I bought a mobile phone and also entered a barber's there and had most of my long brown hair cut off. New start, new look, I thought as I walked back to the car rubbing my head.

Madrid's commuter belt seems to reach as far as Guadalajara, about thirty miles to the east, and the flatlands beyond that small city are mostly cultivated. It's only after crossing the bridge over the southern tip of one of the group of reservoirs collectively and poetically named The Sea of Castile that one really enters Spanish Lapland. I stopped to eat in the village of Córcoles and rather than the fixed-price lunch I'd been looking forward to I had to settle for the bread, ham and cheese I bought in a small shop. Apart from an old man and his dog sitting in the scruffy square I saw only the lady who served me. A sign of things to come, I reflected, as I'd been here before and knew what I was letting myself in for.

My village, which I would reach an hour later, isn't quite as desolate as Córcoles, because it has a bar as well as a shop, and as I drove into hillier country along the decent road my sense of anticipation began to mount.

"Bye bye, Glasgow, hello wilderness," I crooned to the tune of the Everly Brother's song, humming the rest of the words which I assumed life would fill in for me later. The forests in the sunshine filled me with something approaching joy and I felt glad that those irksome final weeks with Nicola were finally over. The trees became sparser as I approached the village, but it was pleasant countryside all the same and my views would be far better than those from the maisonette in Hillhead, Glasgow. I was born and raised in the small town of Hawick in the south of Scotland and city life had never really suited me.

The village lies nestled against a small ridge and though almost all the roofs are red, the houses are of various colours; white, off-white, ochre, dull red or bare stone like mine. Many of those in a good state of repair are summer homes and I was pleased to see that mine had now joined that select group. The stonework had been pointed and the wood-framed windows were new. I parked up and walked away to inspect the roof. There had been many loose tiles but now there were none, and the tile-topped chimney stack had been rebuilt. I went to find Pablo, the builder, to get the new keys.

It was about half past seven and the sun was low in the sky, making the other houses on the roughly asphalted street look even more dilapidated than usual. Pablo's neat house is near the large, sombre church on the other side of the village. His wife immediately answered my call through the open door. I cleared my throat, keen to put into practice the Spanish I'd been studying all winter with the only two people from the village I knew at all well, as the helpful, avaricious estate agent was from Molina de Aragón, the great metropolis of three thousand souls some thirty miles to the north.

"Hola, Pilar," I said, extending my hand.

"Jack, you're here at last," the plump woman cried, grasping my hand and pulling me down to kiss my cheeks. At just over six feet tall I'd felt extremely lanky the previous summer in that land of mostly short, older people, but my soft voice and rather bland face seemed to put folk at their ease.

I grinned. "Yes, I am here, Pilar."

"With less hair."

"Sí."

"And no Nicola."

"No, as I wrote in my email to your son, she and I are now separated," I said, selecting one of the stock of phrases I'd prepared earlier, several of them concerning Nicola.

"I know. So are you sure she won't be coming?" she said slowly.

"Sure."

She wrinkled her nose and placed her hands on her wide hips. "Then we'll say no more about her."

"Gracias, Pilar. I prefer that."

"Sit down there and I'll get you a glass of beer. Pablo won't be long."

"Gracias."

Pilar and Pablo are in their late fifties and their two daughters have lived in Madrid for many years. They both married men from elsewhere and had children. They visit at Christmas and Easter and stay for longer in August, overlapping for just a day as the house isn't big enough for them all. Their son, Juan Carlos, married one of the few local girls and they live on the next street. He works with his father but isn't satisfied with his lot. As the primary school closed some years ago, his wife has to drive their two young daughters to school in another village several miles away. In two years' time the older child will start secondary school, which will mean a much longer drive to Molina de Aragón.

Juan Carlos doesn't plan to stick around for so long and intends to move the family to Cuenca, some fifty slow miles to the south, thus completing the exodus of another generation. I didn't know all this at the time, but I'm telling you now because quite soon I'll be too occupied relating the goings-on in my own life which I couldn't have dreamed would occur as I sat there sipping my beer.

Pablo arrived, asked me about Nicola, and I trotted out my line.

"Ah," he said, his round, benevolent face creasing into a sympathetic grimace.

"But we aren't going to talk about her," Pilar said.

He nodded and looked relieved as he took his glass of beer. "You'll have dinner with us now."

"No gracias, Pablo. I have bought food."

He shrugged, before telling me as slowly as he was able that he and his son had placed a bed in the best room and a few more sticks of furniture in the living room, but that most of it was still stored in the outhouse along one side of the rear patio.

"We thought you and… you would wish to buy new furniture."

"No, I will use the furniture I have."

"Muy bien." He slapped his dusty thighs and stood up. "Come on, I'll show you how the new boiler works and the internet they installed and other things."

I stood up. "Vale. Gracias por la cerveza, Pilar."

"De nada. Here you are in your own home, so come whenever you wish," she said, possibly a little aggrieved that I'd declined their dinner invitation.

"Gracias." I smiled. "I am happy to know you and Pablo and I look forward to meeting the other people in the village."

"It won't take you long."

I don't consider myself to be the typical taciturn Scot, but I wasn't feeling at my most sociable just then. Writers tend to spend a lot of time alone anyway, but as well as getting on with my fifth crime novel I wished to ease myself into my new life and get to know my neighbours in my own time. I wanted to work, walk, read and reflect on the drastic turn my life had taken, rather than becoming immersed in a round of invitations which I'd feel obliged to return. That's what I thought that night anyway, as I lay in bed after finishing off my bread and cheese. By going to the shop and the bar and chatting to people in the street, they'd soon get used to having me around. I'd be able to ascertain who might be likely to disturb me while working and who would respect my privacy.

Little by little, I thought as I got out of bed to turn off the light.

3

The next morning I threw off my two blankets – one of which I'd had to fetch on waking up shivering at three o'clock – and went to open the window. It was warmer outside than in, but there'd be time enough to think about heating the place in winter, as I had more pressing matters to attend to. In my crime novels I spare the reader most trivial details in order to get down to the usually gory and unpleasant subject matter, and although in this account there'll be no violence and only occasional minor unpleasantness, I see no reason to change my style all that much.

It was a Tuesday. By Thursday evening I'd arranged the furniture I required and made two trips to Cuenca; the first to buy all the bits and bats I needed and the second to get the ones I'd forgotten. I also did a huge shop in order to fill my cupboards with imperishable food and the old freezer with meat, fish and vegetables. I'd have preferred to buy my food locally, of course, but the single shop had little stock and all of it expensive. I'd buy bread, milk and fruit there and drive to Molina to do subsequent shops, I decided when I strolled down to the bar for the first time on Friday morning.

I was pleased to find it open and unsurprised to be the only customer. It was about half past eight and the smell of disinfectant suggested that it hadn't been open for long. As there was no-one to serve me I strolled around the small, shabby place, whistling softly and perusing the glass cabinet on the bar. Like me, the owner appeared to have settled for mostly imperishable food. There were tins of anchovies, tuna and similar things, but the only fresh offering was a small tray of Russian salad in the refrigerated part of the cabinet. I scraped a stool into position and sat on it. I might have whistled all morning had a wiry man of about sixty not opened the door, nodded at me, and shouted 'Paco!' at the top of his voice.

"Paco is a little deaf," he said to me, tapping his ears.

"Ah." I slid off the stool. "I am Jack. I live here now." I held out my hand.

He shook it firmly. "Ah, you and your wife have bought the old Garrido place, no?"

"Perdón?"

"The house." He sketched one in the air. "You and your wife have bought that big house."

"Ah, yes, but she and I are now separated. I have come to live here alone."

He nodded and glared at the bead curtain behind the bar. "Paco!" he bellowed. "He thinks I have all day to wait for my coffee," he added softly.

"Eh, what's up, Toni?" a big, bald man boomed as he swept the curtain aside and stomped in. A blue tracksuit top stretched over his belly and I caught a glimpse of the slippers on his feet. "You don't need to shout."

The man glanced at me and grinned. "You have a new customer today, Paco."

I introduced myself and we shook hands over the bar.

"Welcome, Jack. Didn't I see you and your wife here last summer?"

"Yes, but she and I are now separated. I have come to live here alone."

He shrugged. "I'm sorry. You speak good Spanish now."

"Only a few phrases."

He nodded. "Café?"

"Sí, un cortado, por favor."

He turned to the coffee machine and Toni asked me what I was going to do here.

"I am a writer. This village is a good place for writing."

"Did you hear that, Paco?"

"Of course I did. What do you write, Jack?"

"I write crime novels."

He turned and slid our coffees onto the bar. "You won't get much inspiration here. We don't have crime and most of us are too old to start now," I think he said. They speak quite clearly in that part of Spain and the hours I'd spent watching Spanish programmes online seemed to have paid off to some extent, as the previous summer I'd only understood the most basic things. Nicola and I had visited Spain a few times – Cantabria, Asturias, Extremadura, Cataluña and Cádiz – so we'd learnt how to ask for things and make a few comments, but understanding normal speech had always been beyond us.

"The village was more... busy last summer," I said.

"Summer is different here," said Paco. "People return to their houses for a few weeks and some tourists also come to stay at the *casa rural*, like you did."

"Sí."

Toni chuckled. "But only you bought a house."

"Ha, sí."

"Have Pablo and Juan Carlos done good work?" Paco asked.

"Very good, yes. New windows, new floors, one new bathroom, new kitchen cupboards, some new doors. A very good job."

"It's a big place for you, isn't it?" Toni said.

I shrugged. "Yes, but I will only use the rooms I need."

"We thought you might make it into a rural lodging house," Paco said. "Such large projects are normally for that purpose nowadays."

I smiled. "No, only for me."

"But you could take guests if you wished to."

"Yes, but I need tranquillity to write."

"That's true."

"Some friends may visit me," I said, although I'd yet to invite any, as they all knew Nicola well.

Toni placed a coin on the bar and patted my shoulder. "Hasta luego, Jack."

"Hasta luego, Toni."

When he'd left I asked Paco what he did.

"He has a little land. He worked in a factory near Madrid for many years, but now he and his wife have returned here. Their children remain in Madrid, of course."

"Do many people come back to live here when they retire?"

"Not many." He shrugged. "Because of the grandchildren, you know." He smiled. "Ha, here we need young people like you, Jack."

"I am thirty-nine."

"One of the younger residents. There are only two young families here now, that of Juan Carlos and another, but they will probably leave."

"How many people live here all the time?"

His swarthy brow ruffled and he made as if to count on his fingers. "About sixty, but a few may not last long." He took two iced shot glasses from the freezer and filled them with a transparent drink. "We need you to find a new wife and have lots of children. Salud."

I knocked back the aguardiente and tried not to gasp. I'm not a big drinker, so it went to my head almost instantly.

"Gracias. Can I have another coffee, please?"

"Of course."

The caffeine and alcohol made me positively garrulous and I was bold enough to ask him how he made a go of it in the bar.

He shrugged. "I don't, except in summer, but if I close, where will people go?"

"That's true."

He went on to tell me that he possessed a lot of land and had made a decent living. When the former owner of the bar had become too old to continue, he'd decided that as he lived next door he was fated to buy it and keep it open. His house now extended over the bar and kitchen, which explained why he hadn't heard me come in, as he didn't appear to be hard of hearing. He then told me that he'd recently given his livestock to his son.

"The livestock but not the land, because if he chooses to leave, he won't have it until his mother and I are dead."

"Is his the other young family you mentioned?"

"Yes, and each have the same problem, schools." He shook his head. "When a village school closes there is little hope for the future."

"How many children do there have to be to keep a school open?" I said, more or less.

"Only five, but one less and that's it, finished, usually forever."

"That is sad."

"It's the way of the world."

"I am sure a lot of people living in cities would like it here."

"And what would they do?"

"Some could work online."

"Do you have internet?"

"Yes, but it is very slow and sometimes… stops."

"We're lucky to have it at all, but there's little investment in this area, for obvious reasons."

"The roads are still quite good."

"Yes, but they're roads to nowhere."

I took out my wallet. "I will go to write a little now."

He waved my note away. "Next time. Just call when you arrive. I don't stay down here in the bar for no reason."

I smiled. "Now you have a new customer."

"I'm glad. I open almost every day. If I'm not here my wife or a friend of mine will be."

"Hasta luego, Paco."

"Adiós, Jack."

4

After strolling back along the empty streets I opened my door and realised for the first time just how enormous my house was. I'd been so busy carting things around and arranging the living room and my bedroom to my liking that I'd almost forgotten about the other three bedrooms and two more rooms on the ground floor. One of those would eventually become my study, lined with the two thousand or so books I possess, but for now I'd write on an old oak table which I'd pushed up to one of the two south-facing living room windows. Anyone passing would see me at work, but I'm not one of those writers who require complete isolation to do my stuff. Back in Glasgow if the phone rang I usually answered it, but as my new mobile only worked beyond the upper edge of the village I wouldn't need to worry about that. If a neighbour passed by I would wave cheerfully and maybe even nip outside to greet them, but up to press I'd seen no-one, as my house is near the end of the street and beyond it there are only two shuttered houses before the scraggly fields begin.

I dusted the table before opening my writing laptop and placing my notebooks beside it. I took out the post-its from one of them and stuck them along the left-hand edge of the table. I opened the document containing my manuscript and saw the post-its gradually peel off and one flutter to the floor. I had no option but to rewrite those essential notes onto new post-its and stick them symmetrically into place. I was putting off the fateful moment when I would read through the seventy-odd pages of the first draft of my fifth novel, my entire production during the last nine months. It normally takes me about a year to write a book and my publisher was expecting my new one by November at the latest, so I had five months of hard work ahead of me. I patted my post-its, made a cup of tea and began to read.

Crime novels tend to be quite formulaic and as the fourth had gone down well I wished my detective, who I'd be employing for the second time, to go through the same sort of motions in pursuit of a similar class of potential villains. This kind of writing isn't exactly high art, but it works for many famous authors who know what their public want and give it to them year after year. My first two books had been quirky flops, my third more conventional, and my fourth the standard fare which my publisher – and my readers, it turned out – had wanted all along.

I scrolled down and re-entered the seedy streets of my city of choice. My man had just left his office, not dissimilar to the one which Philip Marlowe had worked from about eighty years ago, and was going to buy some cigarettes. I looked at the hillside across the valley and groaned. Was this why I'd become a writer? To churn out standard stuff for fifty-books-a-year crime and thriller readers who might get round to mine after reading all the big-hitters?

"This is your work," I said aloud, and went on reading.

An hour and a half later I closed the laptop. It wasn't too bad, after all. I'd even felt moments of enthusiasm on rereading certain thrilling or eloquent passages. I'd already chosen my villain, but what if it turned out to be him instead? That would really surprise folk and I'd only have to change a few things I'd written so far. I opened a new notebook and sketched out a writing schedule that would enable me to finish the first draft by the end of August. A thousand words a day, six days a week. A piece of cake. I occasionally wrote as many as two thousand words in a day, especially when there was lots of dialogue, so I'd get ahead and free up time for when the summer crowd arrived. After cunningly readjusting my schedule to enable me to start on Monday instead of Saturday, I covered the table with a large towel and went off to the shop.

I'd visited the small grocery store twice the previous summer and despite my shorn head the thin, middle-aged lady recognised me and enquired after my wife.

"She and I are now separated. I have come to live here alone," I said with great fluency.

She frowned. "Oh, I'm sorry to hear that. Is she all right?"

She's shacked up with the bloody doctor who sneered at my sperm, I thought but didn't say.

"Yes, she is well and will stay in Scotland. I have come here to write my books in peace."

"Yes, it is peaceful here," she said with a wistful smile.

"But in summer more people come, no?"

"That's true. We all look forward to the summers."

"I'm Jack. Pleased to meet you."

She smiled. "I'm Encarna."

Just then an aged lady clad in black shuffled in, so after nodding to her I asked for a baguette, a litre of milk and the single bag of apples on the shelf.

"Unless you want them, señora?" I said to the old lady, using the formal mode of speech which I hadn't bothered with until then.

"I can't eat them," she croaked, not seeming especially pleased to see me. Maybe she was too old to worry about the future of her village, I reflected, or she just didn't like the look of this tall, slim, pale man with a severe crew cut.

"The fruit van comes on Mondays," Encarna told me.

"Ah, good. I will buy apples, oranges and bananas every week."

"He also brings vegetables."

"I will buy those too. Potatoes and carrots and… other things."

She smiled. "Then I will bear that in mind when he comes."

"Gracias. It is good to eat fresh fruit and vegetables," I declared sagely.

The way the old lady stood resting both hands on her stick and peering up at me suggested she didn't have time to hang around all day while I waffled on, so I paid, bade them good day and walked out into the hazy sunshine. The shop was on one side of the small village square, so I sat down on a stone bench beside a trickling fountain and counted my change. I realised that my weekly fruit and veg bill was likely to be substantial, but I would keep my promise and refrain from stocking up when I went to the supermarket in Molina. One had to do one's bit to keep the shop going, after all, I was thinking when I saw Encarna strolling towards me.

"I forgot to tell you that another van with the meat and fish comes on Wednesdays."

Shit, I thought, my €40 per week shopping budget is going right out of the window.

"Ah, good." I decided to be honest. "I didn't know that, so I have a lot of things in my freezer, but I will buy meat and fish from you in future, Encarna."

She chuckled. "Be sensible and only buy the things you need. I don't rely on the shop so much, thank God."

"What do… does…?"

"My husband has a lorry. He drives all over Spain. The shop keeps me occupied."

"It is good that the village has a shop and a bar."

She shrugged. "It's lucky that Paco and I wish to keep our establishments open."

"What will the people do if there was no shop?" I said, as I still struggled with conditionals.

"Vans go to the villages with no shops. Different vans which have counters and sell to the public. Mobile shops really, but even more expensive than mine."

I sighed. "I suppose people have to go to Molina to do a lot of things."

"Some things, but there is a post office, pharmacy and health centre in Beteta."

"Oh, how far is it from here?"

"About twenty minutes in the car."

"Much closer than Molina. Do any buses come here?"

"There is a bus to Molina. Now I think it passes twice a week, but that may change. From Beteta there are buses to Cuenca, but you have a car, don't you?"

"Yes, but I was thinking about the people who don't have one."

She shrugged. "They stay here."

"What if they get ill?"

She laughed. "Ambulances do come here, you know. Even helicopters have been known to go to some villages in winter when they were cut off, but none have come here yet. For appointments one of us normally drives them to Beteta if the doctor or nurse cannot come here."

"Ah, good."

She chuckled some more. "You're very curious, Jack. Are you going to write a book about us?"

I shook my head. "No, I only write crime novels, in places in Britain." I glanced at a dusty Seat Ibiza down a nearby street. "Is there a garage for cars here?"

"A garage? For what? One can park anywhere."

"No, I mean to repair cars."

"Ah, you mean *un taller de coches*. No, our mechanic is Salvador. He also repairs tractors." She tapped her nose. "But not officially, you know, only for cash."

"That's good." I'd made sure that my car insurance included breakdown cover, but I'm pretty hopeless with mechanical things and had bought only the most basic tools. "I will speak to him. Look, a lady is entering your shop."

She chuckled. "Yes, Fridays are always very busy. That lady is here for the weekend with her family."

"Do you have more family here?" I said as we walked towards the shop.

"My son is in Barcelona and my daughter in Vienna."

"Vienna in Austria?"

"Yes, she works for the diplomatic service. My son is an accountant."

"They must be very clever."

She smiled. "They had a good teacher here, one of the last, then stayed in Molina at my sister's house when they went to secondary school. After that they studied in Madrid. They've worked hard and we're proud of them."

"Yes... yes. Do they often visit?"

"At least twice a year. In summer they stay for about two weeks." She stopped on the threshold, closed her eyes and faced the sun. "Ah, summer is only a few weeks away now."

"Yes, I'm looking forward to it. Hasta luego, Encarna."

"The van comes at about ten on Monday. Adiós, Jack."

Back home I ate a tasty apple, ignored my shrouded writing desk, and decided to go for my first proper walk. With a sandwich and a bottle of water in my knapsack I began to climb the ridge to the north of the village, only to find that the track ended a short way into the pine woods. I pressed on regardless for a while, but when the prickly bushes drew first blood from my pale legs I turned back and tried another route to the west. I would soon discover that proper footpaths scarcely exist in the area, so I had to rely on rough tracks and the overgrown paths that I guessed hunters used to use, judging by the corroded cartridge cases I came across now and then. That day I zigzagged here and there, happy to be alone in the woods, apart from the birds and the odd rabbit, and I got home sweaty and slightly sunburnt, as I'd neglected to apply the cream I'd bought.

5

After a shower, lunch and a short siesta I paced around the empty rooms for a while, before going to the bar to see if there was a Friday evening crowd. I found Paco dressed more smartly and wearing shoes, with Toni and two more men seated at the bar.

"Hola, Jack, we're very full, but you may come in," Paco said cheerfully.

They were all drinking small bottles of beer, so I ordered one before greeting Toni.

"Hola, Jack. This is Miguel, who has come all the way from Zaragoza to see us, and Juanjo, who is lucky enough to live here."

I shook hands with the two fifty-something men and was glad they didn't enquire about my wife, as I recognised them from last summer. Although they both wore casual clothes it was clear that Miguel was the city slicker, due to his shiny shoes, fine watch and neat haircut. It was Juanjo who was more inclined to talk, however, and he asked me about the work on the house, what I was going to do with all those rooms, if writing crime novels paid well, and if friends of mine would be coming to visit. In short, he gave me a friendly inquisition without mentioning my wife, so I assumed that Paco, or maybe even Pablo the builder, had told him to avoid the subject.

After I'd answered his questions as best I could they resumed their discussion about football. On being asked, I told them I was a Rangers fan, despite having no interest in the game whatsoever, but as they knew none of the players – and nor did I – they soon returned to the Spanish soccer scene while I looked on, nodding appreciatively and trying to keep up with their rapid beer drinking. Although the bottles were small – just 20cl. – after four or five I began to feel tipsy.

"You English like the beer, eh?" said Miguel, whose damp, highly coloured face suggested that he'd had a few before I'd arrived.

"I'm Scottish, but yes, I like it, though I don't drink a lot."

"Perhaps you prefer wine," said Paco, producing a bottle of white from the fridge in one seamless movement.

"No, gracias. Beer is fine."

He flicked the top off another bottle and I vowed to make it my last. I wished to ingratiate myself with the locals, but didn't mean to wake up with a hangover. Besides, it was preferable for them to know the real me from the word go, so I was planning to shoot off when Miguel looked at his watch and tapped his glistening forehead.

"I have to go." He drained his bottle and tossed a note onto the counter.

Toni and Juanjo realised that they too ought to make tracks, as it was nine o'clock and almost dinner time. I stood up, but the patting motion of Paco's hand made me slide back onto my stool. After hearty farewells until the morrow, the door creaked shut and we were alone.

I smiled and swirled the beer in my bottle.

"Would you like to have dinner with my wife and I?"

"I..."

"She asked me to invite you if you came in."

I resisted an impulse to make some lame excuse and gratefully accepted his invitation.

Within two minutes he'd wiped the counter, pulled down the shutters, flicked off the lights and was leading me through the tiny kitchen and up a new staircase. We walked through a spartan sitting room with wicker furniture and a small television into the house he'd lived in all his life, he told me. Past the upstairs rooms and down an elegant wooden staircase I was surprised to see a huge, open-plan kitchen, dining and lounge area. His wife closed the oven and turned to greet me.

"María Jesús, this is Jack, our new neighbour."

The trim, attractive lady of about five feet seven – slightly taller than her husband – pulled off her oven glove and held out her hand.

"Hola, Jack, I've heard a lot about you already," she said in a pleasantly low, clear voice.

I pressed her hand lightly and smiled. "Nothing bad, I hope."

"Ha, not yet. Everybody is glad to have the first permanent newcomer for a long time."

I remembered the grumpy old lady in the shop. "I am glad. I am a quiet person and I will try to be a good neighbour."

"And I believe you write?"

"Yes."

"I'm a keen reader, but please sit down. I'll serve dinner in a moment."

I joined Paco who was already at the table munching olives and almonds.

"Wine?" He tilted the bottle of red.

"Just a little, please."

He filled the small glass. "It's good that you aren't a heavy drinker, Jack."

"Oh, why? I mean, I know it is bad, but..."

"Because of our isolation, especially in winter. Those who console themselves with drink come to a bad end. Salud." We clinked glasses and sipped. "Everything in moderation, eh?"

"Sí." I ate some crisps.

Presently María Jesús brought over a casserole dish and then bowls of potatoes and vegetables, before serving each of us.

"Another day I'll prepare some typical dishes of the area such as *morteruelo* and *atascaburras*, though they're really more suitable for winter. As I wasn't sure if you were coming I've just prepared a little lamb."

I tried a bit. "It's delicious."

"Do you cook, Jack?"

"Only basic things, but I try to eat healthy food."

"Did your... did you eat out a lot in Scotland?"

"Sometimes. My wife cooked quite well, but I also cooked sometimes," I said, as I didn't wish Nicola to become a totally taboo subject, not among friendly folk like them.

"Tell me about your writing?" she asked as Paco shovelled in the tasty grub. I already suspected from the way she spoke that María Jesús was more cultured than her husband and our subsequent book talk confirmed this. After I'd confessed to being a mere crime writer, she referred briefly to P. D. James – one of the more literary luminaries of the genre – before we discussed writers such as Faulker, Melville, Flaubert and Proust, all highly accomplished authors who aren't the easiest to appreciate. I'm fairly well-read for a crime writer, as are many of the really fine ones, and I was impressed by her knowledge of foreign literature.

"And you must also have read all the great Spanish authors," I said.

"Oh, yes, and I'll be happy to lend you any of my books that you wish to read."

I glanced at the bookcases. "Thank you, but Spanish literature is still too difficult for me. I am still studying my grammar books. Do you read much, Paco?"

He wiped his mouth with his napkin. "The newspapers."

"Ah."

María Jesús patted his arm and chuckled. "Paco likes to pretend to be a philistine, but he isn't really. When I was studying literature in Barcelona many years ago he used to borrow a good book from me every weekend and read it before we next met, didn't you, dear?"

He shrugged. "I had to prove I was worthy of you. Once we were married I could drop the pretence."

"Did you come to live in this house when you married?"

"Yes," she said. "And you're probably wondering what I did with my studies."

"Well, yes."

"I became a housewife and I've never regretted it. We wished to have children, so how could I become a teacher or something and be posted many kilometres from here? Besides, I didn't really study with a vocational objective in mind. I loved literature and still do. Have your novels been translated into Spanish?"

I almost choked on a potato. "Excuse me. Oh, no, my sales are not high enough for that."

"María Jesús could help you to translate one of your books," said Paco.

I sniggered. "Oh, I'm sure she wouldn't want to do that. They are just simply written crime stories for the average modern reader."

(My Spanish hadn't suddenly improved, by the way, but I won't subject you to my multiple errors.)

"There's nothing wrong with writing clearly and you shouldn't belittle your own work, Jack," she said gravely.

"Do you read in English?"

"I'm afraid not." She chuckled. "Castilian is my only language."

"My books aren't for readers like you anyway. My... publisher always makes me take out any difficult words." I shrugged and sipped my wine. "I must go on writing these books, as I have to make money."

"That's right," said Paco. "We cannot always do exactly what we wish to, and simple people like me also have a right to read books."

María Jesús laughed and shook her head, before beginning to clear away the plates. Paco stayed put, but I stood to lend her a hand.

"Please sit down, Jack. I'm only going to put them in the dishwasher."

She brought the fruit bowl and plates and as I peeled a banana I confessed that I had to force myself to read crime novels, especially new ones, in order to keep in touch with the public's taste.

"For me I wouldn't read many of them, but I must see what kind of things other authors are writing."

"What are you reading at the moment?" she asked me.

"Well, I have all of Tolstoy's books on my tablet, so I'm rereading some of those."

"Even when he became a religious nut he was a fine writer," said Paco.

"You see?" María Jesús said to me.

He chuckled gutturally. "But Lee Child is much better than him."

"Oh, my God, the things he says!"

Paco grinned. "Am I right, Jack?"

"No, but Lee Child is very good at what he does. He has a formula and it has worked very well for over twenty years." I shrugged. "He's rich."

"Do you wish to become rich, Jack?" she asked.

"It would be nice, but it's not so important to me. Just to make a living from my books is enough for me. If I become established perhaps I will write a crime novel every two years and have time to write other things too."

"Will you need much money to live here?" Paco asked.

"Not so much," I said, before struggling to explain that although my house was paid for, Nicola still had a modest mortgage on the Glasgow house, so despite her high salary and her family's wealth I would still feel obliged to send her some money every month.

"Sorry my Spanish is so bad," I concluded, surprised that I'd been so forthcoming with them.

"We understand you," María Jesús said as she stood to fetch the coffee.

Paco clicked his tongue and patted the table. "But if her family are wealthy..." He shrugged.

I went on to explain that Nicola was a lawyer and had always been the main breadwinner.

"Why did you split up?" he asked.

"Paco, don't be so nosey."

"She met another man, a doctor," I said, refraining from telling them that my sperm had brought them together, awful as that sounds.

"Ha, well that scoundrel can help her to pay the mortgage then," he said.

María Jesús patted his shiny head as she passed by. "Don't interfere with Jack's life, dear." She sat down and filled our cups. "It would be good if you could find time to write things that you really want to. We only live once and one must try to have a fulfilling life. For me, to read and reflect on the works of others is usually enough, but if you're a writer, you must be true to yourself and write from the heart."

"You could write about the village, when you know us better, of course," said Paco.

"Ha, Encarna at the shop asked me about that, but I wouldn't wish to."

"Why not?"

"Well, it seems too intrusive to write about real people."

He shrugged. "Change the names. A foreigner's perspective of our isolated lives might be interesting."

"Even if Jack did decide to write something of that nature, he wouldn't be able to do it for some time. When will you finish your next crime novel?"

"By October, I hope."

"Then work hard to finish it and then try something different. Perhaps something from your own experience that you feel strongly about," she said.

This two-pronged attack ought to have made me feel uncomfortable, but it didn't, as I liked them and felt that they had my best interests at heart.

"Yes, I think I will do that. I sometimes think that if I only write crime stories I will lose the ability to write more… deep things."

"I'm sure some rich bestselling authors look back on their careers and wish they'd tried to write more accomplished books too," she said.

"A few of them, yes," I said, because as they wallowed in their pools in the Bahamas or wherever I guessed that most of them felt pretty pleased with what they'd achieved. "After ten or twelve books I suppose it is hard to change, especially when you get used to selling a million each time," I added, now totally uninhibited about my awful grammar, and also, it turned out, what I said with it. "Is your family from here, María Jesús?"

"Yes, for many generations."

"This wilderness can still produce a few clever people, eh?" said Paco.

I smiled, "I just wondered. Encarna's children must also be clever."

"Yes, but her ancestors cheated." He raised his bushy brows comically. "Her real grandfather was purportedly a Jewish man from Russia who passed through this area, selling clothes, I believe, but they don't talk about him much, as her grandmother quickly married a local farmer, or so the story goes."

"It may not be true," said María Jesús.

"There are many great Jewish writers," I said.

"Yes, like Neil Diamond."

María Jesús chuckled and the two of us began to discuss Kafka, Saul Bellow, Philip Roth and others until Paco could no longer stifle his yawns.

"Ah, this simple man needs to sleep."

"I will go now. Thank you for the delicious meal."

"You're welcome. Why don't you come next Friday too?" she said.

"I'd like that, thank you."

"I hope your writing goes well this week."

"I think it will."

6

The next morning I decided to get on with my novel after all, as a long day stretched ahead of me and there'd be time enough for a good walk later on. That way I'd be ahead of schedule, which I always find soothing in case I get stuck and need to take time out to rethink things. María Jesús was largely responsible for this burst of enthusiasm, of course, as she'd made me reflect on where my writing life was heading. Unlike many of my colleagues I'd enjoyed teaching English at the secondary school on the outskirts of Glasgow, but I'd left that rewarding job to pursue my true passion. At first I'd imagined that I'd ease my way out of the crime genre – depraved characters and their gruesome deeds help a new novelist to get himself noticed – but I had instead toed the generic line in my quest to make it pay.

Still, my work in progress wasn't at all bad, in its way, and after reading it again I tentatively tapped out a couple of sentences before strolling around the house while my coffee brewed. This wandering from room to room had become something of a habit and I began to wonder if subconsciously there was more to it than simply a means of stretching my legs. Perhaps I ought to fetch some of the furniture to give the rooms a bit of life, I mused, and I would have guests at some point when I got around to inviting them. On entering the larger empty room downstairs I decided to bring in the old easy chairs and a few other things from the outhouse, but not before writing at least five hundred words, as this sudden furnishing bug was little more than procrastination.

The prolific fantasy and science-fiction author Ray Bradbury used to have a note pinned on the wall above his writing desk which said simply 'Don't think!' This may sound like a strange motto for someone engaged in any kind of brainwork, but the principle was that the ideas must be allowed to flow and that by deliberating over every phrase one was likely to get bogged down and make little progress. On returning to my desk I decided to take a leaf out of his book, not by writing 'Don't think!' on a post-it and sticking it on the window, but by getting stuck into my story and seeing what I came up with.

About an hour and a half later I saved the document – for about the fiftieth time – and went to pour myself some more coffee. On reading it through I expected it to be pretty poor, as I'd never given myself such a free rein before, but apart from several minor mistakes I found it to be quite good. I'd written an astounding 1,364 words and my character – not the detective, but another one – had done something I hadn't planned at all. I read it again and smiled as I closed the laptop, feeling like a schoolboy who'd just cheated in an exam.

Could I really write like that, or had I just got lucky? After my walk, shower, lunch and siesta I sat down once more, reread it, and blazed away for another two hours before stumbling out onto the rear patio, feeling a little lightheaded. A while later I read my day's work through twice – all 2789 words of it – and made a decision. I would go on writing speedily for a week, revise it thoroughly, then send the whole manuscript to my agent. I ought to have almost half the book done by then and she'd be able to tell me if it was any good. If she noticed a sharp descent into gibberish after page seventy – and I knew she'd tell me in no uncertain terms – I'd scrap all the new stuff, put it down to experience, and plod on as I'd always done.

Over supper I went online and typed 'fast writers' into the search engine. After waiting patiently for my chosen page to open I discovered that Ishiguro had written *The Remains of the Day* in four weeks. He'd recently won the Nobel Prize, and although I didn't expect to be considered for that accolade any time soon, it was certainly food for thought. I read on. Robert Louis Stevenson had penned *The Strange Case of Dr. Jekyll and Mr. Hyde* in three and a half days, before rewriting it just as quickly after his wife had burnt it in a huff. *The Boy in the Striped Pyjamas* took John Boyne two and a half days to write. Those fine works would have been polished up later, of course, but ought I to make gallons of coffee and stay up for two or three nights to get mine finished? No, that would be overdoing it, but what I'd read proved that when a writer is truly inspired the ideas just come pouring out. I closed the laptop. I'd give it a week.

I stuck to my new plan, as I'm a stubborn devil when I have a mind to be, and apart from buying my fruit, veg and bread at the shop and visiting the bar a couple of times, I wrote like a demon until Friday lunchtime. 20,237 words in seven days. Not a patch on the above-mentioned efforts, but a heck of a lot for me. In the afternoon I read it through, made some corrections and emailed it to Samantha, my agent. I then showered, put on a decent shirt and went to the bar, prior to dining with Paco and María Jesús.

"Finished?" said Paco, as I'd told him what I was up to.

"Not finished, but I have done a lot." I took a swig of beer. "But it might be no good. We will see."

It was nine o'clock and Toni and Juanjo had just left, he told me, before introducing me to the only other customer, a lean, tanned man in his forties with a curious quiff atop his otherwise closely cropped head.

"Enrique has remained in the village to keep his mother company and works at a bank in Molina," Paco told me.

"That is a long way to drive every day," I said.

"I have a little place there, so I often stay over, but I'm always here at the weekends," he said in a deep but slightly effeminate voice.

"Ah, good."

"What do you think of our little village so far?"

"I like it a lot."

He smiled. "I'm glad. I'd better go now." He held out his hand. "I hope to see more of you."

"Yes, me too, of you."

No sooner had he stepped outside than the shutters went down and we were soon tramping up the stairs.

"Is Enrique gay?" I asked.

"Yes, but don't tell his mother that," he said with a chuckle. "He leads a separate life in Molina. He's had a partner for the last few years, but can't bring himself to tell her as she's almost eighty now."

"She must know."

"I suppose she suspects something, but we've never had an openly gay man in the village and he doesn't want to be the first, though when she passes away I imagine that will change, as other people have seen him in Molina with his partner, a man called Adán."

"The older people here will probably be surprised," I said as we walked down into the living area.

"What do you think, María Jesús?"

She looked up from the sofa and closed her book. "Hola, Jack. What's that, Paco?"

"About what Enrique will do once his mother is no longer with us."

"In what sense?"

"Regarding Adán."

She shrugged and took off her reading specs. "I assume they'll come here at weekends and in the holidays."

He rubbed his beefy hands together. "Ooh, what a scandal that will be for the old folk."

I pictured the old crone with the stick who I'd seen in the shop. I hadn't laid eyes on her since, but she often popped into my head and had even played a bit part in a dream. Perhaps she symbolised something, or her sour face had just stuck with me.

"The old folk will soon get used to it," she said. "Gay people have stayed in the rural lodging here before, after all."

"Yes, and I remember the looks those two men from Madrid got as they walked along the street hand in hand," he said, finding the subject amusing.

María Jesús stood up and walked over to the kitchen. "Please excuse my husband, Jack. He isn't very enlightened in some ways."

I chuckled.

"Eh, each to their own is what I say, but you must admit that the people here are old-fashioned."

"They're just old," she said, before telling me that the dinner was to be totally traditional. "I thought I might as well make several typical dishes so that you can try them. I shan't make any of them again before the winter."

"Gracias, María Jesús."

Over our *atascaburras* (potatoes with cod), *morteruelo* (a kind of gooey pâté), *zarajos* (lamb intestine wrapped around vine twigs), and *migas con huevo* (fried breadcrumbs with bits of meat and a fried egg on top) we talked about several things. Paco had told her about my week of uninhibited writing and she thought it might work well, as long as I was truly inspired and not just hammering away at the keys like a man possessed with an urge to finish the book.

"If the writing has to be straightforward and the ideas keep coming, why not go on? But you'll have to revise it thoroughly, of course."

"Yes, I will. I'll see what my agent says." I sipped my red wine. "Tell me, is there any kind of initiative in this area to get people to move here?"

They glanced at each other. María Jesús laid down her fork and dabbed her mouth. "The regional politicians talk a lot about what they want to do in the area, normally just before election time, but so far we've seen no real action. In Teruel, south of here, they've done more. They've tried to improve services to encourage people to stay and have also actively encouraged young families to settle in the villages, with the promise of work, but I'm not sure how successful that has been."

"I read that in a similar region in Italy one village is paying people €2000 to move there, and also giving them cheap places to rent," I said, glad that we'd got off the subject of writing so soon.

"I read that, and also something about another village in Italy where they've taken in a lot of refugees," said Paco. "That has proved to be quite controversial, I believe."

María Jesús glanced at me. "Do you not think that's a good idea, Paco?"

"Yes, to some extent, as it's good to help the refugees, but to fill one village with them isn't the answer. That village will lose its identity and become a different place."

"Paco isn't keen on some foreigners, Jack, but he's being diplomatic in your presence."

"I'm not a racist, but some areas of Madrid now look like an African country. I believe immigrants should be encouraged to assimilate, not take over *barrios* and push the local people out. You mentioned Teruel. Well, I read in the paper that in one small village there a Moroccan family moved in. He has a job on the village council, looking after the place, and their two daughters are settled at school. They all speak Spanish now. *That* is a good thing, not a great influx into one place."

"So would you like a young Moroccan family to come here?" she asked him, a smile playing on her lips.

"Yes, if there was work for him and a school for the children, why not?" He shrugged. "Bah, it's too late for this place now."

"If, for some reason, two or three families came here, with a few young children, would the school reopen?" I asked them.

"I suppose they'd have to reopen it, as that's the law," said María Jesús.

Paco smiled. "Why do you ask, Jack? Do you have a plan?"

"Oh, no, but in Britain more people now work from home. With good internet one can do a lot of things. In Scotland there are many islands. They have a similar problem, with young people leaving to find work, but there are a lot of… initiatives to get people to go and live on them. There has been some success." I shrugged. "Do young Spanish people not like to have a new challenge? I know there is still a lot of unemployment here."

"Young Spaniards look outwards rather than inwards, as they've done for many years," said Paco. "Just like in the 1960s, people are going abroad to find work."

"Yes, I have seen Spaniards working in Glasgow," I said, having had a chat with one young man in a cafe there. "And in London there are thousands, I believe."

"Ah, if only some of them saved money and came home to repopulate the villages, but that is just a dream," said María Jesús. "The modern Spaniard is increasingly urban in outlook. Here a person who leaves is considered successful, while one who stays is seen as a failure. I get the impression that northern Europeans are more advanced than us in some ways. Their eyes are more open to new possibilities. Look at the number of them who come to retire in Spain. It wouldn't occur to a Spaniard to go to live in another country if it weren't to better themselves economically."

Paco pushed away his empty plate and raised a thick forefinger. "And when young people do show initiative here, look what happens."

"What?" she said.

"Fraguas."

"Oh, yes, have you seen the news on television this week, Jack."

"Not this week, no," I said, although prior to beginning my writing blitz I had occasionally switched on the ancient TV set to get some listening practice.

"Well, to the north of Madrid a group of young people have taken over an abandoned hamlet. They've rebuilt some of the houses and planted crops. The hamlet was completely abandoned, you understand, but unfortunately it lies within a designated natural park area, so the regional government is taking them to court. Not only will they have to leave, but they will have to pay the costs of the demolition of their work and may even end up in prison."

"In prison? What for?"

She shrugged and Paco snorted. "Technically they have committed a serious offence," he said. "And as Spanish politicians only think of lining their pockets, they'll allow the judicial process to take its course. What do they care about half a dozen idealistic young people? There are *hundreds* of abandoned hamlets and villages in Spain, but instead of encouraging initiatives of this kind, they wish to make an example of them. It's true that they may have chosen the wrong place, in a natural park, but former residents who now live in nearby villages have shown their support. *They* wish to see their old home come to life once more, but the politicians do not. This is what we're up against, Jack."

He jabbed his finger at me, having become quite heated. "Someone like you arrives here and those of us with a brain in our head become quite excited. You alone give the place a little more life, so imagine if you settle here and have children. Imagine if friends of yours arrive and buy another house. The few local youngsters will begin to see their village in a new light. If these wealthy foreigners come, it must be a good place, they'll think." He chuckled and sipped his wine. "You, my friend, may be just the tip of the iceberg, eh?"

María Jesús clapped softly and smiled. "Bravo, my dear."

She began to clear the table and despite her protests I got up to help her, because if I were to be the village saviour I felt I oughtn't to sit idly by. Perhaps it was the three glasses of wine I'd drunk, but Paco had inspired me and as I stacked the plates in the dishwasher my mind was awash with vague ideas. When we sat down to eat some fruit I tried to articulate my thoughts. (Just this once I'll try to show you what my Spanish really sounded like at that point.)

"I think first it is important for people to come here to visit with idea to live here. The *casa rural* we stay in is expensive, a lot of luxury, but one not meet local people."

"There's always the bar," Paco said, pointing at the wall.

"Yes, it's true, but me and… Nicola we come, we look, we drink something, but not talk. Busy then with summer people, so hard for us. We went home, have jacuzzi, and think, oh, this is nice holiday place. Tomorrow we go to another *casa rural* somewhere. All very…" I tried to think of a word like quaint, but failed. "… fun, but only for a week."

María Jesús chuckled. "But you're contradicting yourself, Jack. The two of you bought a house, after all."

"Yes, well…"

"I see his point though," said Paco. "Them buying a house was a minor miracle, a thousand-to-one chance, and if I'm honest I'd say that the fact that your relationship was beginning to fail might have made you take that extraordinary decision, in order to… revitalise things."

"To give us something to think and talk about, yes."

He shuffled on his chair and clasped his hands on the table. "I think that to attract potential residents we need, first of all, to… not exactly advertise, but announce that houses are available cheaply in a quiet village set in nice countryside and with reasonably good roads."

"Do you expect people to come and buy an old house like Jack did?" María Jesús asked.

"Ha, that would be ideal, but it's too much to expect. No, my idea is for them to be able to rent a house or maybe part of a house cheaply and stay here for a while. This time of year is ideal, as we have the whole summer before us. They would meet a lot of villagers, both residents and those who only come back to visit, and see what kind of place it is."

"And in winter, then what?" she said.

"Ah, well, that will be the moment of truth, of course, but it's very pretty here when the snow has fallen. Anyway, for people from the north of Europe it will be nothing new for them."

"So are you thinking of foreigners rather than Spaniards?" I asked.

"Jack, the Spaniard has always been influenced strongly by foreigners, both for bad and for good. Until not so very long ago Spain was a very backward country. I'm only sixty-one, but I remember the furore caused by the foreign tourists when they first arrived on the coasts in large numbers. Look at their clothes, look how freely the women behave, we said. Maybe we're missing something, we thought back then when Franco had only just died. Anyway, my point is that maybe the foreigners have to show us the way, as you are about to do."

I laughed. "I have no idea how I'm going to get on here."

"You'll get on fine. Are we having coffee, dear?"

"Sorry, I was transfixed by your enthusiasm, Paco." She smiled at me. "Until you arrived he only grumbled about the demise of the village, so his argument is valid in his own case at least."

As she made the coffee a hush fell while we each mulled over what we'd discussed. To change the subject now would be an admission that we'd been spouting so much hot air, so as I stirred in a single brown sugar cube I asked them if it would be possible for a few of us to renovate an old house.

Paco smiled. "How do you foresee that happening, Jack?"

"Well, the house would have to be cheap, even cheaper than mine was, and we'd renovate it in a basic way, not at all like the rural lodging, but just a humble village house. Once it is finished we could announce that it is available for those who wish to try living here for a while. They would pay a modest rent, so we would recoup some of what we had paid." I looked at their pensive faces, wondering if they'd understood my appalling Spanish.

"Go on," said Paco.

"That's all. It's just an idea."

"And a good one, but I fear that few people would be willing to contribute," María Jesús said.

"Hmm."

"Would you be prepared to contribute, Jack?" Paco asked me.

I ran my hand around my slightly sweaty neck. "Yes, I… yes, I think I can," I said, as the audacious idea of asking Nicola if she'd mind going a few months without my mortgage contributions had occurred to me. The payments were more a question of pride than necessity, and when we'd still been planning to come here together – until about December, I seem to recall – we had discussed the bigger picture and wondered if others might follow our example.

"Paco and I would also contribute, but I don't know who else would, and we aren't in a position to spend many thousands of euros."

"Me neither."

"The idea is good, but it would take time to put into effect," said Paco. "Given time I might be able to persuade some of my friends to subscribe to our noble cause, but we also have to find the house and get the work done." He smiled. "I'll look into it, and maybe this time next year we'll be in a position to invite people to stay, God willing."

What I said next made me wonder if María Jesús had spiked my coffee, but of course she wouldn't do such a thing.

"There are many rooms in my house."

"That's true," said Paco.

María Jesús frowned. "You have your writing to consider, Jack."

"Yes."

Paco had closed his eyes and appeared to be sketching something in the air.

"Are you all right, dear?"

"Hmm?" His eyes sprang open. "Oh, I was just picturing Jack's house as it was before he lived there. Did Pablo leave the rooms as they were?"

"Yes. You must both come to see me sometime. I will make a meal. Most of it looks quite empty now."

"Which is your bedroom?"

"The one at the front of the house, next to the bathroom."

"Of course, that makes sense. So, there are three empty bedrooms upstairs, one at the front and two at the back."

"Yes, and two empty rooms downstairs, though the smaller one will be my study eventually. It seems a shame to have so many empty rooms, especially after what we have been talking about."

"The house is big for you, but you must have peace to write," she said.

"That's true," he said. "That's your livelihood, so you mustn't be disturbed."

"Oh, I don't mind a little noise, as long as people don't interrupt me."

"The bathroom downstairs has a bath and a shower, no?"

"Yes."

He smiled. "Well, at least if family or friends of yours come for any length of time they won't disturb you. They can use that bathroom and you could furnish a sitting room downstairs for their use."

"I was thinking of doing that. You seem to know the house well, Paco."

He smiled. "I was good friends with Fede Garrido when we were boys. I played there a lot. Then his father became a policeman in Valladolid and they left. Over the years they came less and less and when both of Fede's parents had died, he and his sisters decided to sell." He shrugged. "The same old story. It used to be such a busy, happy house too."

I pictured the bare, echoey rooms. I imagined what it would be like to have a lodger, or maybe a couple. They could use the back bedroom furthest from mine and the downstairs bathroom. They could have their own sitting room. Only the kitchen would be shared.

"I think I could have people in the house without them disturbing me too much," I said.

María Jesús tutted. "Don't be hasty, Jack."

"Yes, one thing is to have an idea, another thing is to put it into practice," said Paco. "Perhaps our plan to renovate an old house would be better."

María Jesús refilled our coffee cups.

"Gracias. Hmm, but if I invite people to stay for a limited time – one month, for example – we would see how they…

adapt to village life. If they like it and want to live here, then we could help them find a permanent place, if they are the right sort of people."

"But what if they prove to be a nuisance and disturb you? You're in the middle of a book, remember," she said.

I nodded, wondering if Samantha had read my story yet.

"If they proved to be a nuisance I would personally drive them to the airport," Paco said. "But you must word your announcement carefully, explaining that it's not a cheap holiday, but a project to attract new residents to the village."

"Yes..."

"I think you ought to sleep on it, Jack, possibly for several nights," said María Jesús.

"Yes."

"Will you be writing tomorrow?"

"No, I think I will wait until my agent gets back to me." I chuckled. "I might have to rewrite the work I have just done."

"I doubt it, because you seem confident that it's good."

"Could we call round to see you tomorrow?" Paco said. "I'm curious to see the house and if you're not writing it might be the best time."

"Of course. Please come for lunch... but what about the bar?"

"Do you remember Juanjo, who came in with Miguel from Zaragoza?"

"Yes."

"He will look after the place for a couple of hours. People usually come for a drink before lunch, then for coffee afterwards."

"Won't he want to have lunch with his family?"

"He's a single man. I'll make him something to eat before we leave."

"Shall I bring something for lunch?" María Jesús said.

"No, I will make something. It won't be like your cooking, but I will make something. Thank you for making all those delicious dishes," I said, patting my stomach.

"You're welcome. Now you know how we survive the winters up here in the hills."

I soon took my leave and on arriving home switched on the laptop. The internet was working but there was no word from Samantha. I went to bed and after imagining the presence of others in the house and feeling a slight chill in my feet I soon fell asleep.

7

I got up early and took my coffee and roll onto the rear patio, where I'd placed the scruffiest of the many chairs in my possession. I looked over the rebuilt rear wall at the wooded hills to the north and wondered when Samantha would get back to me. If she was satisfied with my work it would make me feel more inclined to follow up last night's proposal, as I'd have more time to spare for my hypothetical lodger or lodgers. Besides, I'd done most of my research for the novel and if I kept up that blistering pace I'd have the first draft finished within a month. I'd then leave it for a while, thoroughly revise it four times, and Samantha would send it to my publisher in October. Then I'd try to write something interesting for once in which not a drop of blood would be spilt, unless someone happened to accidentally cut their finger. If Samantha's happy, I'll be up for this daring scheme, I told myself more than once.

By half past eight it was already quite warm and I felt that summer was finally in the air. It was early June and in a couple of weeks the seasonal residents would begin to arrive. A few mothers and children would spend the whole school holidays in their village homes, my friends had told me, while their menfolk would come for three or four weeks. Other families would come for shorter periods, but the village would be buzzing all summer long, especially when the *casa rural* – which sleeps up to six people – was occupied. I stepped inside to check my emails, but there were none. A while later I went to the shop to buy bread, milk and vegetables. The old crone was there and she smiled at me, unless it was a grimace, and Encarna asked me how I was getting on.

"Muy bien, gracias."

"Pilar was asking after you."

"I'm going to see them this morning," I said, as I'd only seen the builder and his wife twice and it was about time I paid them a visit. Besides, there was something I wished to run past them before my first ever guests arrived for lunch. I nipped home, took some pork chops out of the freezer, and strolled over to their house. Pilar ushered me in and indicated an easy chair by the clean, empty wood-burning stove, before explaining that Pablo and their son Juan Carlos were working in a nearby village.

"What are they doing there?" I asked, as I'd been wondering what they had lined up after working on my house for so long.

"Some minor reforms on a house. They're very busy now, as it usually occurs to people to get work done before they arrive for the summer. They'll work every single day this month, then it'll go quiet until the autumn."

"Do they sometimes have no work?"

She shrugged. "Oh, there's always something to be going on with, as they're the best builders around, but jobs like the one on your house don't come up very often."

"No, I suppose not. It would be good if more people came to live in the village, don't you think?"

"Soon they'll begin to arrive." She beamed. "And in August my daughters will come. Ah, how I look forward to August."

"Yes, it will be lovely." I thanked her for the cup of coffee she gave me. "It would also be good if people bought some of the old houses and came to live here all the time, no?"

"Like you and… like you. Oh, it is good to see a new face." She wagged her finger at me. "Though we've seen too little of you, but it would be too much to expect others to come. I mean, why would they want to live here?"

"Well, I came because it's a good place to write, so I suppose other people who have an independent way to make a living might also come."

"What, more writers?"

"Possibly, or artists, or people who do crafts, or those who have some kind of business that they can carry out on the computer."

"Hmm, my son tells me the internet isn't good here."

"It is slow, but it could be improved."

"Well, I'm sure we'd be happy to see people like that coming to live here." She chuckled. "Especially if they give my husband work."

As I was testing the water, I decided to do so more thoroughly.

"Of course, some other people might like to come who aren't so… independent. People who might need some work, or even… er, refugees, from Syria or somewhere."

She raised her eyebrows briefly and smiled. "I'm afraid there's little work here. People who have land work it themselves. They couldn't afford to pay wages."

"And a family of refugees, perhaps?"

Still smiling, she said that it would be far too cold for them in winter.

I dropped the subject and we made small talk until I'd finished my coffee, and as I strolled home I reflected on her response to my speculative comments. I didn't really expect to host folk with no means of making a living, and one can't invite refugees without official intervention, but I'd wanted to see how a typical village lady felt about our idea in all its potential scope. I chuckled to myself as I walked along the deserted street. There I was, still unsure if I wanted a single suitable lodger and already envisioning a dynamic model village, an example to all of how rural repopulation could be achieved. Who was I kidding? I'd most likely get cold feet before I'd even worked out how to entice anyone to my home, and once I resumed my writing – especially if Samantha gave me the green light – I'd probably be too busy to spare a thought for anything else.

"You're looking happy today," María Jesús said when they arrived at just before two.

"Please come in. Oh, you needn't have brought the wine, but thank you."

They looked around the bare hallway and I told them that lunch would be served once I'd fried the chops and boiled the broccoli, as the potatoes and carrots were already done.

"Did your agent contact you?" she asked me.

I smiled. "Yes, she is very pleased with my work. She says it is… fresh and dynamic and that the reader will be turning the pages with... anticipation."

"That's great. Does she know you wrote the last part so fast?"

"No, and as I wrote so little last winter she was worried that I had… er, we say a block of the writer."

"A mental block, yes."

"So she is happy I am now making good progress," I said, before telling them that I'd written back to tell her I'd have the first draft ready for her to see within three months, as she needn't know that I was now one of those speedy scribblers you sometimes read about, often after they've died.

"That's good news, Jack," said Paco. "It takes the pressure off you. Can we see the house before we have lunch?"

"Of course. You lead the way."

As we walked from room to room Paco brought the Garrido household back to life once more. He and his pal had often played in my future study, and young Fede's bedroom had been the one I'd earmarked for my lodger.

"Ah, we'd sit on his bed just here and look out of the window at the hills, planning what we were going to do when we grew up." He sighed and smiled. "He wanted to be a pilot, while at that time I wished to be a civil guard, because I liked the olive uniforms and the strange hats they wore then. It was ironic that Fede's father becoming a policeman took them away from here."

"Did Fede become a pilot?" I asked.

"No, an insurance salesman. He married a girl from Valladolid and there he's remained. I met him when they came to see about selling the house, but I doubt I'll see him again. He has severed his ties, like so many others."

"It's a shame," I said.

"It's the way of the world. If you wish to furnish this room, I'll help you to fetch the furniture. No doubt I'll recognise Fede's bed, unless they got rid of it."

"Most of the beds are old. I'm using the hardest mattress. The others are all soft."

"We're thinking about changing ours," said María Jesús who, with her greying hair in a ponytail and dressed in a stylish blouse and blue jeans, didn't look like the other village women.

"Are we?" Paco asked.

"Yes, it's six years old. It's still decent, but it's time we got a new one." She looked at me. "If you have a double bed frame, you could use the mattress here, for when you have guests."

"Gracias, Pilar."

We toured the remaining upstairs rooms and Paco pointed out that the position of the staircase meant that my guests wouldn't disturb me if they descended while I was in my room.

"Paco, please stop dropping hints about what we discussed last night."

"I was thinking about his friends and family," he said softly.

"I doubt my parents will come here," I said. "My father has arthritis and my mother doesn't like flying. I'll have to go home to see them. My sister and her family might come, but not this year."

"And friends?" he asked.

I screwed up my slightly burnt nose. "Not this summer. They all know my wife and I don't want to talk about her yet. Let's have lunch."

The pork chops fried in olive oil with a little garlic turned out all right, and while eating at the scruffy dining table in the large kitchen we talked mostly about my writing. Although María Jesús was a great reader, she hadn't met a published author before, so I think her interest in my methods and the publication process was genuine, but I also suspected she was trying to keep Paco off the subject of our Lodger Project.

"… so when I receive the final version I have to read it very carefully, even though others have already read it," I droned, while Paco gazed out of the window at the sunny street. "Now that printing is digital, errors can be corrected more easily, but in the old days thousands of copies would be printed right away, and if there were errors the books still had to be sold."

"Yes, I've noticed that modern editions often have no mistakes at all," she said.

"That's right. I'll make some coffee and we'll go into the sitting room."

"Do you mind if I wander around the house again?" said Paco after finishing the last of the wine.

"Of course not."

María Jesús insisted on washing up, and as I dried the plates I told her I'd decided to go ahead and look for a suitable lodger.

"You should resume your writing, then decide," she said. "Once you're working you might realise it isn't such a good idea after all."

I chuckled. "You seem to know what it's like to be a writer."

"Oh, not really. I've written some poetry and a few short stories over the years. Even Paco doesn't know about most of them."

"I'd like to read some of your writing."

She sighed. "If I'm not satisfied I don't show it to anyone, and I'm rarely satisfied."

"That's how serious literary authors tend to be. They write and rewrite and take a long time to finish a book, sometimes years, but the genuine ones have to do this before they are satisfied. That is real art, while what I do is more like producing a… product to sell."

"I'm sure it isn't so different."

"I think it is. If you write about crime there are a lot of ways to… excite the reader, but if you write about real life it is much more difficult to say something original. Ha, Raymond Chandler said that if you don't know what to write next, have a man appear with a gun in his hand. That is what crime writing is like," I managed to convey.

"But Chandler was a great writer in his way."

I ceased to rub the plate. "Yes, I agree. I think he wasted his talent by writing only about crime, and drinking far too much."

She chuckled. "And you think you're wasting your talent by writing about crime too."

I shrugged. "I don't know if I've got any real talent. Maybe I should have continued to teach and just done my writing in my spare time. That way I might have written one good book by now, instead of four... mediocre ones."

"It isn't too late to change, Jack. Make this book a good one, then write something else. You won't need much money to live here, and in winter you'll have no distractions whatsoever."

"Unless I have lodgers."

"Yes."

"But if they don't invade my space it won't matter. I often look out of the window when I'm writing, hoping that someone will pass by."

"In summer a few will, if they're going for a walk in the country."

"I wonder if those two old houses are for sale."

"One may be, but the other will be occupied in August."

"Really? It looks abandoned."

She chuckled. "When Ana has opened the shutters and cleaned the windows it'll look better. They live in Tarragona, on the coast south of Barcelona."

"So some people went to Madrid, others to Cataluña?"

"Yes, Madrid is nearer, but there has often been more work in Cataluña. I'll finish these while you make the coffee."

Paco was waiting for us in the sitting room, perusing an old copy of *The Observer* on the tatty sofa.

"Is that interesting, dear?"

"Yes, I'm looking at the pictures. Ah, coffee."

I pulled an ancient table nearer to the sofa and the easy chair. While María Jesús poured, I went to fetch a bottle of brandy I'd bought for such occasions. Paco poured a drop into his coffee, so I followed suit.

"It's a nice space you have here, Jack," he said. "Before it was more cluttered with furniture, but it seems bigger now."

"Yes, I spend most of my time in here."

"It's also good that you have a door into the kitchen and that there's another door from there into the hallway."

His wife sighed. "Why's that, dear?"

"Oh, so that when his friends come they'll be able to use the kitchen without disturbing him while he writes. In and out they will go, while Jack writes on regardless."

I knocked back my bitter brew and laughed. "Paco, later, if you like, we'll try to furnish that bedroom and the room across from this one. I'm almost sure that I want to have a lodger now."

He grinned and rubbed his hands together. "Yes, I'll help. You need to prepare the rooms anyway, for guests."

María Jesús shook her head and smiled. "How do you intend to find a lodger, Jack?"

"Well, I've been thinking about it and I might put something on Twitter."

"What's that?" Paco asked.

María Jesús explained, although she didn't use it herself. I told them that despite my publisher's insistence that I keep my website up to date and maintain an active presence on social media, I was disinclined to waste time touting my wares on Facebook and suchlike. My website was all right, although it didn't get much traffic, and I still used Twitter, as it only took up a couple of minutes a day. I'd usually retweet a few interesting items, then plug my latest book and that was it, but I reckoned that a carefully worded tweet about our project might generate some interest.

"It may be ignored, of course, but people sometimes retweet things like that, so I hope that suitable… candidates might see it," I concluded.

Paco grimaced and raised his hands. "Tweet, retweet, what's all this?"

"The modern world, dear."

I fetched a pen and pad and explained that the announcement would have to be short. Half an hour later, after several nips of brandy, we came up with something that I then translated as follows:

Attractive village in rural Spain seeking creative people to settle here. Several houses available to buy and restore. Cheap lodgings available for trial period of one month. Please message me if interested.

I added a few keywords with suitable hashtags, before translating it back for them.

"That's fine," said María Jesús.

"It's all right, but very short. There are more things we could say," said Paco.

I reminded him about the 280 character limit.

He scratched his head. "Ah, yes, I remember, but how strange to wish to limit how much people can say."

"People have short attention… these days. Besides, I think it says enough. When someone contacts me I will find out more about them."

"You haven't said that we're looking for young people," he said.

"Well, one has to be careful not to appear to be too selective or to discriminate."

He shrugged. "An eighty-year-old man might want to come. What then?"

I chuckled. "He may be wealthy and leave some money for our project when he dies. Don't worry, I will know how to refuse unsuitable people politely."

"If you find someone promising you ought to have a video call with them," said María Jesús. "That way you'll see what they're like, as people are apt to write glowing things about themselves."

"Yes, I could do that, if the internet can… manage it. I will tell them it is bad here and that mobile phones only work outside the village. That will put off some young people, I'm sure, but not the more adventurous ones."

"Hey, maybe a really sexy young woman will want to come, Jack. Then you won't need the other room after all, eh?" Paco said with a leer.

"Don't be vulgar, dear."

On imagining a dialogue with potential recruits, something occurred to me. "I'm thinking that perhaps we should contact the authorities before I go ahead with this, as I appear to be representing the village. Is there a mayor or someone here who we should speak to?"

"Yes, we could have a word with him," she said. "He's a pleasant man, though a little rough, as you'd expect in a small place like this."

"Could you speak to him then?"

"Yes." She turned to Paco. "Does our project meet with official approval, *señor alcalde*?"

He stuck out his lower lip and nodded grimly. "Yes, the village council approves the measure unanimously."

"I... oh, are you the mayor, Paco?"

He shrugged and smiled. "Nobody else would take on the onerous duties involved."

"Almost everybody votes for him, as no-one else wants to make the occasional trips to Cuenca, despite the hearty meals they get there."

"You are a good person for the job though," I said to him. "You did buy the bar when it was about to close."

"Yes, well, I was thinking of persuading Toni or Juanjo to stand at the next elections, as my dear wife says she doesn't want to become the first ever *alcaldesa*. However, now that we might have something worthwhile to do, maybe I'll continue." He sipped his drink and raised his forefinger. "On a more serious note though, I don't wish to involve the provincial or regional authorities in this at all. I want it to be an initiative of the village for the village. I want to show them what can be done without pleading for subventions and generally kissing arses."

"Don't drink any more of Jack's brandy, dear."

"No." He slapped his stout thighs. "So, shall we move a little furniture now?"

"All right."

When they left at about seven I had a shower and rested for a while, before revisiting the lodger's – or lodgers' – quarters and viewing their transformation through fresh eyes. The bedroom was as austere as mine, but the new sitting room looked quite complete with an old three-piece suite, a small dining table and four chairs, a bookcase and an ornate sideboard. A large rug which I would hoover in due course provided a touch of snugness and I felt pleased with our work. I looked out of the large window at the patio and the hills and decided to have a go at rendering the breeze-block walls on two sides of the patio one day – the outhouse being on the other – to make the transition from the terracotta tiles to the trees and the sky more harmonious.

After a bite to eat I posted the tweet before reading through my recent writing. Later on I viewed the stats and saw that only about a hundred people had seen it. No-one had bothered to retweet it, so I copied it, deleted it and posted it again, just like I did with my book plugs. I intended to do that every day from then on and if no-one contacted me within a week or two I'd have to think of a better way to attract lodgers, such as an ad in *The Guardian*, among whose readers – all raving lefties, my Dad said – there might well be folk who were up for a sojourn in a part of Spain which hardly any foreigners visited.

I went to bed feeling tired but rather pleased with myself. We'd set the ball rolling and now it was up to intrepid individuals to answer the call.

8

The next morning, before beginning to write, I translated the lodger tweet back into Spanish, checked that I hadn't forgotten any accents, and posted it alongside the English version. Paco's conviction that foreigners would be the catalysts of the village's resurgence oughtn't to prevent Spaniards from coming to stay, and perhaps a youngster who was all set to go to work in a cafe in London would come here instead and... do what? That would be my first question when someone got in touch, as they must come with some sort of occupation in mind or it would be a waste of time. My job was writing, so I put these thoughts aside and got down to it.

During the next fortnight when I wasn't hammering away at the keys I think I met most of the permanent residents, either in the streets, square, bar or shop. To describe them all would be tiresome and, quite frankly, irrelevant to my story, so I'll introduce them if or when they play a part in it, although I will say that they were almost all polite and welcoming. My friends' new mattress arrived six days after our fateful lunch, so Paco and I carted the old one round to the house and placed it on my bed, as the one I'd been using wasn't quite as good, but fine for lodgers, we agreed.

"Any response yet?" he asked.

"Only a sculptor from Flagstaff, Arizona who says he might come next year. I will do the tweets for another week, then think of a different way to announce our project."

"Yes, because we don't want the summer to go by without anyone coming."

"No."

He sat on the lodger's bed and sighed. "María Jesús feels that I might have pressured you into this business."

"Not at all," I said, though I knew that his powers of persuasion had tipped the balance.

"Look, if someone comes and they prove to be a nuisance, don't worry. We'll take them in, then I'll drive them wherever they need to go. María Jesús insists that your writing mustn't be disturbed."

"I'm making good progress now. The ideas keep coming and I should finish the first draft in a couple of weeks. Then I will have more time," I said, as I hoped the first lodger would arrive soon after, though that seemed unlikely just then. I often feel quite flat when I finish a first draft and lay the work aside, so a new housemate would be a welcome distraction.

"We could also have someone to stay at our house, of course," he said. "There's my son's old bedroom and another smaller one, but they'd have to share our living space."

"No, you don't want to do that, Paco. Here they will be able to live their own life, or lives."

"That's true. Are you coming for a drink?"

"No, I must get on with my writing."

Apart from my daily walk, shopping, a bit of sunbathing and the odd trip to the bar, I worked flat out for another week, before rereading it all and planning the astonishing and, I hoped, quite original *denouement*. Writing fast seemed to work for me after all, as I found the story to be pacier than my previous ones. On the warm, sunny Monday after I'd just begun the penultimate chapter I checked my emails prior to heading for the woods and found that I'd received my first Twitter message since that of the chap from Arizona. It was just a brief note from a man called Neil whose Twitter account was so new and blank – not even a photo – that I assumed he'd set it up expressly to get in touch with me. His message read:

Hello, Jack. I'm interested in coming to stay in the village. Please email me at...

I snorted. Fat lot of effort he'd put into that, I thought. I sent an email asking him to tell me more about himself, before opening the *The Guardian* website to see how much small ads cost. It didn't specify the price, but it wouldn't be cheap. Maybe I should use my neglected Facebook account after all, I thought as I applied some sun cream, before stepping outside and beginning to see the whole business in a new light. I was prepared to take a lodger in order to do my bit for the future of the village. I had spread the word and got practically sod all response. Oughtn't I to just chill out, enjoy the summer and adopt a laissez-faire attitude towards the Lodger Project? I strode off up the ridge, resolving to continue the tweets but think no more about it.

When I got back two hours later, bathed in sweat and feeling pleasantly purged, I couldn't resist opening the laptop. I found an email from Neil which read as follows:

Hi, Jack,

I live in Castleford, West Yorkshire, and until recently I worked as a postman. I've retired at fifty-five and I'm now thinking about coming to live in Spain. I've been studying at college and speak some Spanish. I'd be interested in staying for a while with a view to buying and doing up a property in the village. I like reading and cycling and also draw and paint a bit, though I'm not very good! I can pay rent, no problem, and would like to come out soon. If you think you might want a bloke like me, please tell me a bit more about the village and yourself.

Cheers,

Neil.

I found myself smiling on reading this succinct but informative missive, until I realised that a fifty-five-year-old ex-postie wasn't really what we were after. After a quick shower I printed it out and trotted off to the bar. To my surprise María Jesús was holding the fort, with only Juanjo for company.

"Hola, Jack! How's the writing going?" he said as he pumped my hand.

"Muy bien. No Paco today?"

"He's with Edu," María Jesús said, referring to their farmer son. "A man has come from Teruel to buy some pigs and Edu wanted his father to be present. He knows how to handle those rogues better than him. A beer?"

"Yes, please. I've got an email from someone who wants to come," I said, waving it in the air.

"Oh, how exciting! Do read it to us."

Juanjo swept back his unruly grey hair and clenched his rather irregular teeth. "Is it a young, single woman?"

"No, it's a… well, I'll translate it."

I did so.

"He sounds like a single, middle-aged man, like me," said Juanjo.

"Yes, I'm afraid so."

"He seems like the right sort of person, if a little older than we expected," said María Jesús. "Do postmen get good pensions in England?"

"Well, as he retired so early it probably won't be more than €1000 a month."

"Oof, that's plenty of money. More than a lot of people earn around here," said Juanjo, who owned some land and kept a few animals, so I doubted that he reached such heady heights very often, but he'd had the good sense to buy the family home from his brother and sister – both exiles – when their parents had died a few years earlier. He was fifty-eight, a lifelong bachelor, and his only indulgence were his frequent trips to the bar, Paco had told me.

I sipped my beer and sighed. "He sounds all right, but he isn't really the kind of person we're looking for."

María Jesús pursed her lips and moved her head from side to side. "Hmm, he isn't young, but on the other hand he's probably solvent and self-sufficient."

"Well, if he owns a house in Yorkshire and decides to sell it, he'll have plenty of money."

"And if he buys a house here and restores it, it'll be a tremendous success," she said. "But perhaps you don't feel like hosting a man of those characteristics."

"Oh, I don't mind. It's only for a month, after all, and nobody else has shown interest. What will Paco think?"

"Oh, he'll be all for it. Fifty-five isn't so old, after all. You could have a video call with him and see what he's like."

"Yes, I'll try to do that. I'd better go and get on with my writing now."

I fumbled for change, but Juanjo flapped one hand and slapped a coin on the bar with the other.

"Gracias."

"De nada. Maybe that Englishman will come here and I'll have someone new to talk to."

Later on I emailed Neil and asked him if we could Skype at eight the following morning, UK time, explaining that later than that the internet usually began to play up. I could have suggested an evening call, of course, but I preferred to see and hear him in the light of a new day. He wrote back five minutes later, agreeing happily and stating his Skype address.

To cut a long story short – for we talked for over half an hour – and in order not to anticipate the delights of Neil before his arrival, I agreed to put him up for a month.

"That's brilliant, Jack," he said in his pleasant Yorkshire accent.

"You'll have to make your own way here. That's part of the deal."

"No hay problema," he said, also in a Yorkshire accent. "I'll be with you in about a week."

"OK, bye for now, Neil."

"Hasta pronto, Jack, y gracias."

"De nada."

9

I then worked harder than ever on my book, as the last thing I wanted was for Neil to arrive while I was still in full creative flow. I'd expected to get further emails from him that week, asking all manner of questions, but I didn't hear a thing until the evening of the day when I'd typed the final sentence. He simply told me that he'd be arriving on Tuesday, the day after next, and was looking forward to meeting me and seeing the village. His timing was perfect, which I felt augured well, as I just had time to read the whole thing through. I was really pleased with it, and rather than the feeling of emptiness that usually assails me on finishing a first draft – as I always file them away for at least a fortnight – I had plenty to do, such as cleaning the house, driving to Molina for some shopping, and buying plenty of fruit and veg at Encarna's shop.

Tuesday, the first in July, was also the first really hot day we'd had, and as I hoovered my three rugs dressed only in shorts I wondered how he would arrive. He hadn't asked me about transport connections, so I guessed he'd catch the train from Madrid to Cuenca and take an expensive taxi from there, unless he got the bus to Beteta, in which case he'd have to contact me. I checked my emails at least once an hour and when I heard a knock on the door at about three I loped down the hall, expecting to see my guest and his luggage.

Instead I found two girls of eight and nine on the doorstep, the daughters of Juan Carlos, son of Pablo and Pilar.

"Hola, chicas."

"Hola, Jack. There's a strange man on a strange bicycle in the village," chirped Paula, the younger of the two.

"He must be looking for you," said Marta.

"Do you mean a motorbike?"

"No, a bicycle with funny bags on," said Paula.

"He looks foreign, like you," said Marta.

"He's very red, like you."

"Where did you see him?"

"Near the church. He was asking Doña Regina (an ancient widow) something, but I don't think she understood him," said Marta.

That Yorkshire accent, I thought. "Let's go and see." I put on a t-shirt, shut the door – I rarely locked it – and the three of us headed off to find the mystery cyclist, who had to be half mad to be riding on such a hot day. I'd seen a couple of mountain bikers around recently, probably tourists staying at the rural lodgings available in several villages, so I suspected it was one of those, but when I saw a fully laden touring bike outside the bar, with panniers fore and aft, plus saddle and handlebar bags, I began to suspect that it really was Neil. We peered through the window and there he was, a tall, slim man with tanned arms and legs, receding brown hair and a big smile on his chiselled face. He held a bottle of beer in one hand and gesticulated with the other, clearing trying to explain something to Paco, who wore a perplexed smile. I'd have liked to have stood there watching for a while longer, but I thanked the girls for leading me to my lodger and pushed open the door.

The squeak made Neil turn and his bright blue eyes opened wide.

"Hola, Jack. I've just arrived."

Paco flicked the top off a beer, looking relieved.

"Hi, Neil." I shook his damp hand. "Have you cycled from Madrid?"

"No, from Bilbao."

"Bloody hell. How far's that?"

"Just over three hundred miles, as I avoided the main roads. I'm a keen cyclist, you see."

"Yes, you must be. Is all your luggage on the bike?"

He gave a throaty laugh. "Some of it. The rest will arrive by courier this week, hopefully."

"Ah, good. Paco here is a good friend of mine. This project to revitalise the village is mainly his idea."

"Yes, you said when we spoke," he said in his deep, jovial voice, before addressing Paco at some length.

"Perdón?" said he.

The trouble with Neil's Spanish, apart from the Yorkshire accent, was that it was a kind of stream of consciousness which omitted most verbs, mangled others, and was almost impossible to understand. *I* knew that he'd told him how he and I had got in touch, how pleased he was to be here, how he already liked the village, and how great Spanish roads were for cycling, but of course I knew the language he was trying to translate from. I'd have to give him a few pointers, but not yet.

I conveyed Neil's message to Paco and he opened three more beers.

"Neil, welcome to our village. I hope you enjoy staying with Jack. Whenever you wish we can speak about the houses that are for sale here," he said slowly.

"Perdón?"

I turned a sigh into a contented 'Ah' before translating.

"Oh, bien, bien. I don't think my Spanish is quite as good as I thought it was. My teacher told me I should just speak and not worry too much about the grammar. I know loads of words, but I'm not that sure about how to put them together," he told me.

"Have you cycled far today?"

"Only about thirty miles, from a place called Molina de… something or other."

"Molina de Aragón. I went shopping there yesterday. Did you camp?"

He chuckled. "No, I've been staying at hotels and hostels. It's taken me five days."

"You must be knackered. Shall we go to the house so you can have a shower? We can always come back here later."

"All right." He took a small purse from the rear pocket of his green cycling top, but Paco ushered it away.

"Gracias, Paco."

"De nada, Neil."

"Hasta luego."

"Hasta luego."

We left.

"You see I'm right enough with simple things like that, but when I try to say something more complicated they don't seem to understand me," he said as he pushed his bike up the street, gazing around him like a curious child and not seeming at all tired.

"Did you bring a grammar book or anything?"

"They'll arrive in my luggage, but to be honest I can't be doing with them. I'd hoped that I'd be able to learn as I went along, just chatting to folk, but I'm not so sure about that now."

"I'll..."

"So I'll get stuck in again when they come and iron out whatever it is that's stopping folk getting what I say. Oh, sorry for interrupting, Jack. I tend to ramble on a bit when I'm excited."

I laughed. "It isn't a very exciting place, I'm afraid, though the summer visitors are starting to arrive."

He stopped pushing his burdensome bike and turned to face me. "Oh, Jack, but it's exciting for me. Since my divorce and finishing work I've decided to embrace life with more passion." His blue eyes sparkled with, I feared, a touch of fanaticism. "This little cycle tour, for instance. Though I've been cycling for forty years, Sunday club runs were always enough for me. When the club went off youth hostelling I'd normally get cold feet and make some excuse. I liked being a postman well enough, but I often felt I should have a change, but I never had the balls to do it. When my wife said we should go to Florida on holiday, I said, oh, let's go to Spain again. She thought I was dull, but I'll show her. Well, I won't show her, because we aren't speaking any more, but I'll show *myself*, which is more important, isn't it, Jack?"

Oh, lord, I thought. "Yes, it is. Er, shall we get out of this sun?"

He pushed the bike. "Ha, yes, there I go again. If I natter on just tell me to put a sock in it. How's the writing going? Did you finish your book?"

"Yes... er, that's to say I finished the first draft. Now I have to go through it again and again until I think it's right," I said, already feeling that a handy alibi to secure solitude would be required.

"Well, I shan't be disturbing you when you're at work, but I do hope we'll be able to spend a bit of time together."

"Yes, of course. Here we are."

"Wow, what a lovely house, and so big!"

"Yes, it's big." I pushed open the door and ushered him in. "Your bike can have a room to itself, as there are plenty of spare ones."

He leant the green Merlin bike carefully against the hallway wall and ran his hands through his short, sweaty hair. "Phew, I'll be glad to see the back of this thing for a while."

"The roads are really good for cycling around here. You could go for miles and hardly see a car," I said hopefully.

"Yes, but I find cycling a very solitary activity. Enjoyable, but solitary, and I want to spend a lot of time in the village, getting to know the folk. It isn't good for me..." his voice trailed off and he gazed at the floor.

"What?"

"Well, when my wife left me it was a hell of a shock and I didn't want to see anyone for a while. I'd get home from work, lock the door, and that was it till the next day. I became quite depressed and ended up having time off work. The doctor prescribed anti-depressants, but I just chucked them away. I preferred to get through it on my own, and I did, eventually." He gazed at me sadly, the sparkle gone. "When I felt a bit better I enrolled for Spanish classes, and once I got into that I was fine again. Most of the other students were nice and we sometimes went out for a drink after class. From then on it's been up and up, and though I still have the odd sad spell now and then, I'm determined to make the most of what life has to offer."

I smiled empathically and nodded. "I see."

He slapped his hips and grinned. "Ha, here I am, boring you with my nonsense already."

"Not at all. It isn't nonsense. I'll show you your room."

"Great."

We grabbed a pair of panniers apiece and I led the way upstairs. He said the room was just fine, the view lovely and the bed comfortable.

"I'm glad you like it. I'll show you your bathroom and sitting room now."

He arched his brows and scratched his large, pointy nose. He wasn't an especially handsome man, but his face was expressive, and I'd already witnessed two widely contrasting moods.

"Mine?"

"You'll see." I led the way downstairs and showed him both sitting rooms. "Me being a writer, I need my own space, as even when I'm not working I might get an idea and start making notes," I said, rather lamely, I feared. "So I might join you in your sitting room if you want to chat, but I'd like to keep mine private... for that reason."

"Fair enough, Jack. Ha, the world of the writer is a closed book to me." He guffawed. "Though I do like reading, as I told you."

"What do you read?"

"Oh, mostly thrillers, crime, true crime, you know. Nothing very intellectual."

During our video call, when he hadn't rambled on too much, I'd given the impression that my writing was a very earnest endeavour, which I suppose it is in a way, so he probably thought I was a brainy literary author rather than yet another commercial hack. I decided not to reveal this for the time being.

"Across here is your bathroom."

He liked it and lost no time in explaining why.

"My wife had me doing DIY non-stop for twenty-odd years, Jack. Once I'd done the bathroom, it'd be time to tile the kitchen or change some cupboards or paint a room. It was a never-ending cycle. The flaming house had to look like new all the time." He patted the old Roca cistern. "It'll be nice to have a bath in here and look at the tiles and think, there's nowt wrong with them."

I chuckled. "The kitchen's been done up a bit. Come and look." I ushered him in.

"Oh, it's a fine kitchen. I'm not much of a cook, but I have got better since I've been alone."

"Well, there are plenty of cupboards, so you could have these two here. Feel free to eat anything you want. I'll go to Molina to shop next week, so you can come and buy the things you like. I use the local shop too, but it's much more expensive." I opened the fridge. "I'll clear some space for you here. The freezer's there in the pantry, so feel free to use that too."

He nodded solemnly and gazed at the fridge door. "Will we... er, eat together sometimes?"

I gulped. I hadn't given this much thought, as when I'm writing I eat when it suits me, but we weren't students sharing a communal kitchen, after all. I thought fast and came up with a plan.

"I've been thinking that we could have our evening meals together, unless one of us goes out. I eat lunch at different times, you see, because of my writing."

His lips curled up and his eyes met mine. "That's great, Jack. I don't want to get under your feet, but it'll be nice to have dinner together and catch up."

I smiled. "Yes, it will. Right, I've got to go and do a few things now, so I'll leave you to unpack and settle in. There's tea and coffee in this cupboard and help yourself to whatever you want from the fridge."

"Thanks, Jack. I'll pay for the next lot of shopping."

"All right. There are towels in your bathroom. The washing machine's in there, next to the freezer."

"Ah, good. I'll pay you the rent later on."

"There's no hurry." During our call I'd told him that the €200 for the month was destined for our project, which reminded me that I'd only agreed to put him up for that length of time. I found this thought soothing. "Anyway, make yourself at home and I'll see you in a while."

"I will, Jack, and thanks again," he said, beaming once more.

10

On closing the door behind me I breathed in the warm air and wondered what I'd let myself in for. Rather than flopping onto my bed for my daily siesta, there I was, out on the street in the heat of the day. There was only one cool place I could possibly go just then and for the first time I lamented the size of the village. One bar, one shop, nothing else, so we could hardly lead separate lives. Rather than going to the bar, as I felt a spell of lamentation coming on, I turned left and headed up to the woods, where I sat down in the shade of the first trees and tried to get my head around my new situation.

My hypothetical lodger had been a youngster with a creative occupation of some description who would be busy all day long and might deign to chat to his host for a while in the evening. He – for I'd envisaged a male – would ask me about my writing and tell me about his painting/drawing/sculpting/pottery/writing, before I returned to my sitting room to watch a bit of telly. Neil, as well as being a rather intense and possibly slightly unstable chatterbox, had nothing specific to keep him occupied. I leant back against the pine trunk and depressed myself further by imagining the worst case scenario.

I'd get up in the morning and there he'd be, at the kitchen table wearing a smile from ear to ear. We'd breakfast together and I'd end up going to skulk in my sitting room, pretending to write, while he pottered around the house, waiting for me to emerge. If I went to the bar he'd find me there. If I went for a walk he'd join me. Coinciding in the house at midday we'd end up lunching together. When I went for my siesta he'd go for his in order to be refreshed for the evening we'd spend together in his sitting room, before turning in early so we could do the same again the following day.

Right, that's just about as bad as it could possibly be, I thought, so how could I go about making it better? I almost wished I was still working on my book, because I had no desire to start something else and it was too soon to begin to revise it, but he needn't know that. Maybe if I retired to my sitting room after breakfast he'd toddle off around the village and amuse himself chatting to the locals. Once he'd recovered from his trip he might go cycling after all, which would keep him out of the house for several hours. He may decide to spend a lot of time in the bar, so then Paco would have to bear the brunt of his loquacity rather than me. He'd told me he drew and painted a bit, so hopefully he'd trot off to do that for hours on end. He said he liked reading too.

I pushed myself to my feet, resolving not to be such a whinging pessimist. Occasionally I'd felt lonely in the evenings and had dwelt on the happy years I'd spent with

Nicola. Now I'd have company if I chose, and although Neil was an odd and potentially bothersome man, I was a writer after all, and ought to jump at the chance of getting new material. I'd only agreed to a month-long stay anyway, during which time the plan was for him to look into buying a house, so that too should keep him occupied, and Paco was the man he'd have to ask about that. I put on my cap and set off home, but found myself walking along another street and soon reached the bar.

Toni and Juanjo were at the counter, along with a man I hadn't seen before. There was no sign on the door barring the entry of women, but I'd yet to see a female customer. Juanjo introduced me to Alfredo, a portly chap of about my age who lived in Albacete.

"What made you wish to go to live there?" I asked him, my Spanish having improved quite a bit during the last couple of weeks, as certain intangible linguistic elements seemed to have come together at last.

He shrugged. "I did the state exams for an administrative post and I ended up there. It's less than three hours in the car. I'm here for the rest of this week, then I'll leave the wife and kids and go back to work till August."

"Ah, so is your wife from here too?"

"From Molina, but they like it here in the village. The kids can play out without any danger, and their grandparents will drive over too."

"That's good."

"So how's your guest doing?" Paco asked as he handed me my coffee.

"Fine. He seems friendly and talkative," I said, not about to gripe in front of the blokes, as one of them might hold the key to Neil's future there, literally if they possessed an old house.

Paco smiled wryly at me. "Yes, Neil is very… open, but hard to understand."

"I'll help him with his Spanish."

"No doubt he'll want to look at houses soon."

"I hope… think so. I haven't asked him yet."

"Well, let him settle in for a while before bringing up the subject, eh?"

"Yes, I'll do that."

"A week or so, just to see how he likes it."

"Yes."

"And bring him here," said Juanjo. "I don't care how bad his Spanish is, as mine's none too good."

"I'm not sure that you'll–"

Paco coughed. "Neil could come here before and after lunch, and in the evenings too. Juanjo is always keen to meet new people, so Neil can practise with him."

"Yes, tell him to come," said Juanjo.

Paco turned and winked at me.

I twigged. "Ah, yes, I'll tell him that." I drank up and placed the customary euro on the bar. "I'll tell him now in fact. Hasta luego."

"Really? That's very kind of him," Neil said when I told him that a friendly local man had agreed to give him free conversation classes. I'd found him in his bedroom, unpacked, showered, dressed in civilian clothes and about to hit the town.

"Yes, he's called Juanjo and he's in the bar now, so you could go to meet him, though there are a few more guys there."

"Yes, I'll go now. Are you sure he doesn't want me to pay him?"

"No… no, you'll just be chatting to him really. He's not that educated actually, but I'll give you a hand with the grammar. It's probably best not to think of them as classes at all," I said, not wishing to overstep the mark. "Just chat to him when he's free and with anyone else when he isn't."

He eyed me zealously. "I'll be off then. Would you like to come?"

"I'd better get on with my writing. I normally have dinner at about nine. I'll make something for us today."

"That's grand. I've only been here for a few hours and I'm loving it already."

"I'm glad. Hasta luego then."

"Ha, yes, hasta luego, Jack."

Neil was out for so long that I thought I might end up eating the microwaved lasagne and fresh vegetables alone, but he tapped on the door and walked in at five to nine, looking flushed and happy.

"Sorry I'm nearly late, Jack, but I've been talking to Juanjo for the last hour."

"Ah, good. And before that?"

"Mainly listening." His breath smelt of beer, but he seemed only slightly tipsy. "I didn't understand much, but when I got Juanjo alone I got the gist of what he said."

"He's a great one for gesticulating, isn't he?"

"Ha, yes, that helped a lot."

I stirred the carrots. "Help yourself to another beer, Neil."

"Oh, no thanks. I've had about six of those little ones and that's plenty for me. I kept finding a full one in front of me."

I chuckled. "Yes, that happened to me at first too." I stirred the peas.

"You look a bit concerned about something, Jack. You're not annoyed at me, are you?" he said, looking a bit sheepish.

"Ha, course not." I was pleased that he'd stayed out for so long and appeared to have hit it off with Juanjo and the others. My spell of sulking earlier in the day now seemed unfounded, but I did have something on my mind. "I'm just a bit pensive. I had another Twitter message earlier, you see, from someone else who wants to come."

He smiled, then his eyes seemed to cloud and his cheeks grow slack, before he smiled again, but a bit falsely, I thought. He would have made the worst poker player in the world.

"Oh, that's good news, isn't it?" he said.

"Well, I don't know."

"For the project, I mean. Paco told me a bit more about the project. I think I understood him because me and you talked about it during that video call. It's great that you've got involved in something like that so soon after moving here." The sparkle was back. "It shows what a selfless person you are, Jack."

"Yes, well," I said with a shrug.

"Who wants to come?"

"Let's dish this out and I'll tell you while we eat."

"Shall I grab a can of beer for you?"

"Yes, please."

We dined in Neil's sitting room – so that he'd start to feel at home there, I said – and I told him about the long and informative message I'd received from a young lady called Jenny. It would have been easier to have read the message aloud, but she sounded so perfect for the Lodger Project that I didn't want him to think that I'd have preferred her to him, which I did, on paper at least.

"She's a promising writer from Derbyshire. She's had a few stories published in decent magazines and is in the middle of her first novel," I said in a matter-of-fact sort of way.

Neil sipped his water and nodded. "It sounds like you'd have a lot in common, Jack. How old is she?"

"Thirty-one. She's been living in London, working for a publisher and writing in her spare time, but she's fed up of city life and wants to go somewhere quiet to write." I shrugged. "She happened to see my tweet and dropped me a line."

"Does she speak any Spanish?"

"She says she has a GCSE and has visited Spain a few times. I expect she'll know enough to get by."

"More than me, I bet. Does she want to settle here, like me, or just spend the summer?"

"That depends. She says she has enough money to live for a while, but any longer term decisions will depend on the novel. She thinks the publisher she's working for will take it, and she has other contacts in case they don't, but of course even if it's published it might not sell well." I shrugged. "Writing's a very precarious existence."

Neil nodded, sliced off a bit of lasagne, and chewed ruminatively for a while. I drank some beer and picked at my food.

"Ha, I expect you wish I hadn't come now," he said with a deep, melancholy chuckle as he gazed at his plate.

"Of course I do. I mean, of course I don't. You're here and she's just thinking about it." I waved my fork to catch his eye. "If you ask me she's written too much. Instead of getting in touch and us discussing it, she's sort of laid all her cards on the table. Ha, I bet she'll wake up tomorrow and think no more of it. Writers can be flighty creatures, you know," I said with an encouraging smile.

"When does she want to come?"

"She says she'll be free about a fortnight from now. It appears that she's already handed in her notice at work and at her flat. She'll go home to Derbyshire and will stay there if nothing better comes up, she says."

He sighed. "I didn't know you could write so much in a Twitter message. I only signed up to the thing so I could contact you. One of my classmates told me about your tweet."

I finished my can and smiled. "I think I preferred the way we did it. I feel that she's been a bit too forthcoming," I said earnestly.

"Have you replied yet?"

"No. I'm still thinking about what to say."

He stood up. "I must nip to the loo. I'll get you another beer."

"Oh, I'll get..." but he was gone, fast on his feet for a man who'd cycled three hundred miles in five days.

He took his time coming back, however, and I wondered if he was thinking along the same lines as me. I'd agreed to put him up for a month, so by the time Jenny came out, if she did, that time would be almost up. I pondered on this for a while until I heard the flush of the toilet and the patter of large feet. Then he was back with my can in his hand and a nervous smile on his face.

"Thanks, Neil."

"De nada. Ha, I suppose I'd better start looking into getting a house right away, in case she does decide to come."

I chuckled, having guessed right. "Not so fast, Neil. The month I mentioned isn't written in stone."

"Yes, I suppose I could–"

"Hang on." I opened the can. "The month I mentioned was in case the person who came proved unsuitable. If somebody had come who didn't fit in or disturbed my work I'd have been able to ask them to leave after a month, but you obviously like it here. I imagine you've got the wherewithal to buy a house and I know you're not going to be hanging around here all day."

"I..."

"Besides, even if you do find a house it probably won't be fit to move into, so you'll be welcome to stay here until you can move."

His eyes opened wide and he gazed at me like a grateful dog. Whether I would live to regret my decision to back this particular horse, I didn't know – please forgive my mixed animal metaphors – but only a real rotter would have considered giving the friendly and somewhat insecure fellow the boot just because a loquacious young lady had written.

"Thank you, Jack."

I shrugged, smiled and sipped.

"There are more spare rooms," he said.

"Yes, there are."

"And I don't need a sitting room to myself."

"No, I don't suppose you do."

"Or a bathroom."

"No."

"She sounds interesting."

"Yes."

"And might even be pretty."

"Maybe," I said, as she looked quite attractive in her rather fuzzy profile photo.

"And you'll have a lot in common, being writers."

"Yes. Yes, I'll write back and suggest a video call."

"Good idea."

"At which you'll be present."

"Me? Why?"

"Because she'll have to see the *ménage* she might be forming a part of."

"Ha, it might become a *ménage à trois*," he said with a childish titter.

I laughed. "That's not what I meant, but the house is plenty big enough for three of us. This is getting cold."

When we'd finally cleared our plates Neil grabbed them and headed off to the kitchen. While he was washing up I nipped into my sitting room and sent Jenny a quick email, suggesting a video call the following evening. Back in Neil's sitting room I found him wiping the table and humming to himself.

"I emailed her. Hopefully we'll talk tomorrow evening."

"Ah, good. Well, I'll turn in now. I'm a bit shagged out after all that cycling."

"I'm not surprised."

"Oh, here's the rent money."

I thanked him. "Sleep well," I said in Spanish.

"Tu también. Buenas noches y hasta mañana, Jack."

"Buenas noches, Neil."

11

I hardly saw Neil at all the following day. When I went downstairs at about eight he emerged from the kitchen, all set for a walk.

"I'll go while it's cool, then get some breakfast in the bar," he said, all smiles.

I told him that the ridge to the north was the best place to walk, so off he went. After mooching around the house for a couple of hours I decided to drive to Beteta to take a look at the most thriving village for miles around. The compact place is perched on a ridge surrounded by lusher countryside, and the tidy streets of mostly smart houses give it a prosperous air. Its two grocery stores, two restaurants, pharmacy, post office, health centre, junior school, tiny bank and even a petrol station belie the fact that fewer than three hundred people live there permanently, but of course all those facilities also serve several smaller villages including ours.

After plodding up to the crumbling castle to admire the splendid views I repaired to the restaurant in the pretty square and ate a wholesome fixed-price lunch. I wondered if I – or rather we – ought to have explored the area more thoroughly and bought a house there instead. Beteta seemed to be everything a village should be, but when a party of noisy Spanish tourists arrived for a late lunch I suspected that its prosperity was built at least partly on them. My village was more traditional, authentic and… moribund, but if our project took off we might reverse the trend and who could tell what the future might hold?

When I got home at about four Neil was out, so I had a short nap, went for a walk, and was just out of the shower when I heard him come back at eight. Jenny had written to say that I could Skype her any time that evening, so I trotted down to suggest that we get it over with before dinner.

"That's fine by me, Jack," he said, looking less flushed than the previous evening but equally happy.

"Good day?"

"Yes, a lot of walking and talking. I love it here. I bought some bread from the shop. Encarna's nice, isn't she?"

"Yes, she is."

"There was an old woman there who just leant on her stick and stared at me."

I laughed. "You're experiencing the same things as me. Come on then, let's see what Jenny's got to say."

She answered after a few rings and when she came into focus I saw she was every bit as pretty as her photo had suggested. She had short dark hair, a pale oval face and pleasingly regular features. Judging by her neck and shoulders she was slim too, but I wasn't about to be wooed by her looks, not I.

"Hi, Jenny, I'm Jack." I pushed the laptop. "And this is Neil who's staying with me until he finds a house to buy."

She giggled agreeably. "Hello, Neil."

"Hello, Jenny."

I eased the laptop towards me.

"Hello, Jack. It's funny talking like this to people you haven't met before, especially when there are two of you," she said in that neutral accent which most English provincials adopt after spending some time in London, unlike us Scots who merely tone it down a bit. She had a melodious voice though, so I didn't hold it against her.

I made to push the laptop, but Neil smiled and shook his head.

"So, Jenny, thanks again for your message. The house is a big place that's just been done up, so you'd have a decent-sized bedroom and you'd share a sitting room with Neil."

"Which I wouldn't go into if you were working," he said abruptly.

She chuckled. "I'd buy a desk and work in my room, I think."

"Right… well, what more do you want to know, Jenny?" I said, as I'd told her about the rent and the one-month clause when I'd replied to her message.

She leaned forward and smiled. "Oh, I don't know. Look, you both seem like nice guys, so why don't I just come out for a visit and we'll take it from there?"

"Yes, all right, you could do that."

"Do you want to see the house?" said Neil, his head almost nestling on my shoulder.

"Well..."

"I'll carry the laptop and Jack can talk you through it."

This bit of quick thinking made the rest of our call more fun than it might have been. With consummate care he managed to tour the house, walking mostly backwards, while keeping me and/or the room in question on camera. She liked the look of her empty, front-facing bedroom and I promised to equip it with the best of what was left of the furniture before she arrived. Their sitting room also met with her approval and it was there that we said goodbye until shortly after the fourteenth of July, her last day at work.

She waved, the screen went blank, and we both sighed.

"That went well, didn't it?" Neil said.

"Yes, she seems nice."

"I thought you might ask her about her writing."

"Oh, that can wait. Besides, we'll probably just get on with what we're doing. Writing's hard enough anyway without nattering about it too."

"You haven't got many books here, have you?"

I explained that Nicola was looking after them.

"Do you miss her, Jack?"

I stiffened slightly. "Yes and no."

"I still miss Linda, even though it's been almost three years since she left."

I patted his arm. "Let's fix some dinner and talk then."

So it was that over our beef burgers and oven chips he unburdened himself of the sad story of his wife's elopement with… another postman.

"I thought he was a friend. We shared a round for a few months, in the same van, and we became good mates, so I invited him to lunch one day. A fatal mistake. When he got his round changed I was a bit disappointed, and it wasn't till a year later that I found out why. They were at it behind my back for all that time, then she left."

"I see. Do you have kids?"

"Just one, a lad called Bradley, or Brad. He lives in Wakefield, where his wife's from."

"Are you a granddad yet?"

He smiled. "Not yet, but they're trying. Do you have kids?"

"No, we... didn't want them. What does Brad do?"

"He works for the Environment Agency. He drives around inspecting rivers for pollution and things like that. He's keen on it, so he ought to get on there."

"Will he come out to see you?"

"Well, I'd like him to. I could put him up in that rural lodging place."

"Or here."

"Here?"

"Yes. Look, if you like, tomorrow we'll furnish Jenny's... the room Jenny will stay in, then see if we have enough left to do the other bedroom too."

"You can count on me, Jack."

"And while we're at it we could see about the other downstairs room as well. I think that'll be like a study cum library that we can all use, but I'll have to buy some shelves and put them up," I said, having been overcome by a sudden urge to furnish the whole place once and for all.

"I'll help you with the shelves." He chuckled. "I'm pretty handy after all the DIY she made me do."

I mentioned the walls I wished to render.

"A piece of cake. I can't wait. I mean, I can't spend all day every day nattering to folk, can I?"

"No, you don't want to overdo it."

"And if you have to write, I can get on with the shelves, no problem."

"I've almost finished what I'm doing for the moment, so I'll have time to spare."

He grinned. "I'd like to read it, but I don't suppose you'd want me to."

I affected a grave and erudite look. "No, thanks, Neil. I never show my work to anyone until it's completely finished."

"Fair enough, Jack."

12

The following afternoon we drove to Molina de Aragón, which is no longer in Aragón, but the province of Guadalajara. It's a strangely quiet place set in flatter, drier country, dominated by a fairly well-preserved castle which occupies a low ridge to the north. Although small, Molina is the biggest place for miles around, so it has all the facilities one could desire, including a rather expensive furniture shop. That morning we'd sweated buckets carting things from the outhouse to the bedrooms and future study. We'd kitted the spare room out well enough, but I'd decided to buy a new bed and mattress so that I could put mine in Jenny's room. After ordering them I asked about shelves and bookcases too, but Neil took me aside and uttered some wise words in my ear.

"You've shelled out enough here already, Jack. We should find a joinery place and order some nice planks, and a hardware shop to buy the brackets and things. I'll put the shelves up."

I agreed, paid the man, and he told me the bed and mattress would be delivered the next day. After coffee on a cafe terrace in the pleasant *Plaza de España* we went to a *ferretería* to buy tools, brackets, varnish and other sundry items, before driving to a *carpintería* to order sixteen nicely planed planks. Neil did most of the talking and his vocabulary proved to be quite extensive, so I just chipped in when his singular syntax flummoxed his listeners. Finally we visited a builders' merchant and he ordered enough sand and cement to render the patio walls, plus a few more essential items.

"I'll want to paint them a nice colour too," I said as we climbed into the stifling car.

"We can get some paint when we come back to do some shopping. The rendering has to dry properly first."

"Thanks for coming, Neil. I wouldn't have known where to start without you. How did you know they'd deliver?"

"Oh, it stands to reason. I just assumed it'd be the same as in Britain, and it seems to be."

"Yes, I suppose if they sell to people in all the villages, they have to get the stuff to them." I turned to look at the pile of purchases in the back. "I guess I'm prepared for any eventuality now, and you can use the tools when you get a house. Will you do it up yourself?"

"Oh, I suppose I'll do some of it, but I'll put some work Pablo's way too."

"Ah, did you meet him?" I asked, as Pablo seldom went to the bar.

"Yes, I saw him on the street yesterday. He asked me how I was getting on and if I was going to buy a house." He chuckled. "I'm sure he'd like to see more foreigners around the place."

I started the car, turned up the air conditioning and pulled away. "Yes, but I hope it's not only foreigners who come. I mean, we don't want to turn it into some kind of expat colony. Paco thinks we'll sort of set an example to Spanish people who might follow suit, but I can't see that happening," I said, before summarising Paco's spiel about young Spaniards preferring to go abroad to work rather than using their initiative at home.

He nodded. "Hmm, most people are conformists everywhere, but there'll always be a few who want to buck the trend. It's a question of letting them know there are options out there."

Now that Neil had calmed down after his initial exuberance – caused mostly by nerves, I suspected – I realised that he had a lot of common sense.

"Well, I've stopped posting the tweet in English now, as I think the three of us will be enough, but I'm still posting it in Spanish, just in case."

"Ha, you might end up with a full house."

I remembered that before long I'd be beginning my arduous editing process. "Hmm, that might be a bit much."

"I'd make sure no-one disturbed you, but there's someone else who could put at least one person up."

I shook my head. "Paco and María Jesús's house is too open-plan for them to have lodgers."

He looked over and smiled. "I know, but I don't mean them."

"Who then?"

He chuckled. "Guess."

"I… do you mean Juanjo?"

"That's right."

"Have you mentioned it to him?"

"I've hinted at it, or tried to, as with my Spanish I find it hard to be subtle, but I think if a pleasant young Spaniard came he'd be up for it. Having a lodger might keep him out of the bar too, some of the time."

"Yes, it might."

During the forty-minute journey the landscape became gradually greener and hillier and it felt good to be going home to the tranquil place that so many people had seen no option but to leave.

"So is the Spanish tweet the same as the English one?" he asked me.

"Yes."

"Maybe you should reword it a bit. Look, the village is coming into view! Aren't we lucky to live in such a quiet, pretty place?"

"Yes, we are."

"Try finding an affordable house in the Yorkshire Dales, or anywhere else in rural England now. A tiny cottage would set you back two hundred grand. All those bloody second-home owners are pushing the local youngsters out. Is it the same in Scotland?"

"Not as bad. There are still plenty of normal villages, but the ones within commuting distance of the cities are gradually losing their identity. When a local dies an outsider usually buys their house. Yes, I guess we are lucky to live in a place like this."

That evening Neil went to the bar while I allegedly got on with my work. Instead I toured the rooms, now all filled with somewhat scratched but solid furniture, and felt happier about the way things were going. There was more to life than writing, after all, and as I was ahead of the game I could afford to immerse myself in my role of host to future residents of a place that might one day look more like Beteta than the other ailing villages.

On his return Neil told me that Juanjo was warming to the idea of taking in a lodger.

"Paco saw what I was driving at and started telling him how good it would be for him to have a bit of company. I didn't understand half of what he said, but by the end of it Juanjo was beginning to see that it made sense, partly because it'd put a bit more money in his pocket."

"Yes, Paco can be very persuasive. I've put a big pizza in the oven."

"Great. I'll cook tomorrow evening."

After dinner I opened the laptop and we came up with a better Spanish tweet. This is the translation of the original one:

Attractive village in rural Spain seeking creative people to settle here. Several houses available to buy and restore. Cheap lodgings available for trial period of one month. Please message me if interested.

Which we changed to something like this:

Attractive village in rural Cuenca seeking young Spaniards to settle here. Cheap lodgings available for those who wish to embrace rural life and help the village to prosper. Several cheap houses available to buy and restore. Please message me if interested.

"Yes, that sounds better," said Neil. "Can you put one of those smiley faces too?"

I added a suitable emoji and a Spanish flag, before posting it. Someone retweeted it right away and Neil gasped, but I told him not to get too excited.

"There are about half a billion tweets posted every day, so it's pot luck really. The chances of someone suitable seeing it are very slim."

"But I was told about it, and Jenny saw it."

"True. I'll post it once a day, maybe more. Have you no desire to go cycling yet?"

"Yes, I'm starting to fancy going for a spin, but I've a feeling I'm going to be busy tomorrow."

Neil was right, because not only did his luggage arrive, but also the bed, mattress and building materials. Our nearest neighbour, an elderly man called Matías who lived two doors away, had directed the courier van to our house, so I had a word with him while Neil helped the young driver to unload a surprising amount of luggage. Matías had a frail wife who I'd never seen, and apart from nodding to me in the street he'd scarcely acknowledged my arrival.

I thanked him for showing the man where I lived.

He grunted. "You want to paint that number on the door so they'll see it," he said hoarsely.

"Yes, I will, when I get some paint. How are you and your wife?"

He shrugged and pulled down the peak of his old straw hat. "Living."

"If you need anything anytime, just call," I said, as Paco had told me that their only son and his family had moved to

Germany a long time ago and hadn't visited for at least two years.

"Like what?" he said, baring his ill-fitting false teeth in a rather gruesome grimace.

"Oh, I don't know."

"Two of you in there now, are there?"

"Yes, me and Neil, but there's someone else coming in a couple of weeks."

"Another man?"

"No, a young lady."

He opened his mouth and nodded slowly. "Ah, good," he said in a way that made me suspect that when Enrique finally 'came out' in the village he would be none too impressed.

While I had the grumpy old man's attention I told him that my friend Neil was hoping to buy a house in the village and that the young lady who was coming might also want to.

He smacked his lips and screwed up his leathery face. "You're not some kind of sect, are you?"

I laughed. "Of course not. We're just normal people starting new lives."

"All foreigners?"

"Well, for now, but we hope some young Spanish people will come too. Paco, the mayor, is keen for new people to come so that the village won't die."

He grunted, nodded once, and shuffled away just as the van drove off and Neil came loping up.

"Oh, I wanted to meet him."

"Another time. He's isn't too keen on us. He thought we were a couple, or were founding a sect, or both."

"Oh, well. There's no pleasing some folk."

"I see you've got quite a lot of stuff," I said, looking at the two bulging suitcases, a taped up travel bag and two boxes.

"Yes, I felt I should commit myself."

I chuckled. "What if we hadn't seen eye to eye?"

He shrugged. "I reckoned I could get all my stuff in a small van. If it hadn't worked out for me here I planned to buy one and take off somewhere else."

"Right. Have you sold your house then?"

"It's on the market. Half is for… her, of course, but it's a nice detached, so I'll get a good amount. I've got quite a bit of savings, so there's no big hurry."

"It's very brave of you to take the plunge like this."

"Well, the house has to go and I've no desire to buy a terraced in Castleford." He chuckled. "It's Spain or bust for me."

"Come on, I'll give you a hand."

I didn't get the chance to see what Neil had brought because no sooner had we lugged it all upstairs than the builders' merchant's wagon arrived. The rear patio has a metal door that gives onto a weedy plot of land, so I directed them around the house and Neil, the driver and I managed to drag the two big sacks of sand inside, before we each fetched a bag of cement. The wagon still held a lot of material and the dusty driver explained that he made a tour of the villages mainly to the south of Molina at least once a week.

"There's been a lot of building going on during the last few years," he said.

"What kind of building?"

"Mostly rural lodging houses. Is that what this is going to be?"

"No, just a normal house."

"Are you English?"

"No, Scottish."

"My nephew's in London, working in a hotel."

"Oh, right. Does he like it?"

He shrugged. "He seems to. Nothing for him around here anyway."

When the wagon rumbled away I saw old Matías standing on his doorstep. To my surprise he raised his hand, so I waved. Maybe seeing us engaged in such a manly pursuit had convinced him that we were 'regular guys' after all.

A while later the furniture van arrived with the partly disassembled bed and the mattress.

Is it a *casa rural*?" the driver asked.

"No, just a normal house."

After Neil and I had carted them upstairs we adjourned to the patio to drink a beer in the shade.

"Maybe it's a good thing that the planks aren't arriving till tomorrow," Neil said.

I sighed contentedly. "Yes, we're going to be busy."

"Might as well get the place shipshape before Jenny arrives."

"Yes, we might as well."

13

That night I slept in my comfy new bed, feeling a bit guilty and unchivalrous about having palmed Jenny off with the old one, but as Neil said, she was only coming to visit and we oughtn't to pamper her. When the planks arrived at ten the next day, a Saturday, Neil wanted to begin to varnish them right away. We were cutting a few to size on the patio when there was a knock on the door.

"Pasa!" I cried, as I was holding a plank on two chairs while Neil sawed merrily away.

María Jesús had come to pay us a visit, so we finished the plank and showed her around.

"Oh, the house is looking a little more like it used to now," she enthused.

"Did you know it too?"

"When we were children we all knew each other's houses. There weren't so many of us even then. I believe a young lady is coming to stay?"

"Yes, just for a visit. She's a writer."

"I know, Paco told me. He says you haven't been to the bar much lately."

This was because I'd wanted Neil to find his feet without me, but I assured her that I'd be returning to my old sociable ways now that I'd finished – or finally admitted to finishing – my first draft.

"Yes, you must have a good rest now."

I made some coffee and we returned to the patio, part of which remained in the shade for most of the day. We moved the plank and I made a mental note to get some garden furniture before Jenny arrived, and maybe a few plants.

"María Jesús, I want start look for a house soon," said Neil.

"Ah, good. Paco and I have been thinking about which houses might be for sale."

Neil nodded fervently. "Bien, bien."

"And also about who ought to sell and who ought to keep them, if you see what I mean."

"Perdón?"

"Not exactly," I said, before translating for Neil.

"Well, I don't think any are actually on the market at the moment, as some people are too proud to announce to the world that they need the money that the old places will fetch. Paco has been making enquiries and he thinks that at least five owners will probably sell now," she said slowly with appropriate gestures.

"Sí, sí," said Neil, nodding again.

"None of them live here now, but of those five we think that three of them might possibly come back." She chuckled. "They don't necessarily know that themselves right now, but when they retire we think they may feel an urge to return. Then their children may take an interest in the village and the house, and who knows what might happen? Entiendes, Neil?"

He stopped nodding. "Er, no."

I translated.

"So, we feel that it will be better for the village if these people don't sell. The other two houses, however, are owned by people who are unlikely to return."

"Where are the owners now?" I asked.

"Well, one house, quite near to Pablo and Pilar's, is owned by a man who moved from Madrid to the coast when he retired. He hasn't been back for many years and is unlikely ever to return. We believe he's quite well-off and probably hasn't given the house a thought for a long time, although he's been paying the rates through the bank every year. The other house is the one three doors away from here."

"Next to old Matías's house?"

"Yes, that's the one. Two sisters own that. One has lived in Segovia for years and the other is Encarna."

"Of the shop?" said Neil.

"Yes, the only Encarna here. In fact I called at the shop before coming here and asked her about the house."

I deduced that María Jesús and Paco had decided that Neil was right for the village and the village right for him, and so had begun to find him a house. I felt a bit left out, but then again I had given the bar a miss for a few days.

"Did you get that?" I asked Neil in English.

"Encarna has a house and a sister," he said in Spanish.

María Jesús looked at him and smiled. "Encarna is happy to sell the house. She will ask her sister if she is happy to sell the house."

He nodded. "Bien, bien."

"Might her sister not wish to come back to live here one day?" I asked.

"I doubt it. Her husband is from a village in Extremadura and he wants them to retire there." She shrugged. "For visits here she has Encarna's house, so I don't think we risk losing anyone by the sale."

Neil scratched his head. "So, there are two houses that can be for sale?"

"Yes, you can see Encarna's house, and the other one from outside."

He stood up. "Can we go now?"

She chuckled. "Yes, if you like. Can I finish my coffee first?"

He sat down. "Of course, María Jesús, perdón."

We strolled across the village and took a look at the wealthy man's house first. It was an ample two-storey place – with three bedrooms, María Jesús believed – and the closed window shutters had been warped and dried out by the sun, though the stonework and roof seemed to be in reasonably good repair.

"The last time I entered this house was about fifteen years ago when the present owner's mother died," María Jesús said. "I remember it being a little scruffy inside then, and it hasn't been touched since."

"What is that nice house opposite?" Neil asked her.

"La casa rural."

"I stayed there when I first came," I said in Spanish. "Who owns it, by the way?"

"Yet another emigrant. He lives in Barcelona. He went to work as a plumber there and ended up employing several people. He had the house restored at great expense and his cousin looks after it for him."

I remembered the eager man who we'd taken for the owner. "I haven't seen the cousin since I've been living here," I said.

"He lives in Beteta. You may see him when people come to stay."

"It looks empty now."

"Yes, it often is. There's a lot of competition now and tourists prefer the villages with a little more life. Come on, let's get the keys to the other house from Encarna."

Before handing them over, the shopkeeper stressed that everything depended on her sister. "For me, Neil, you can buy the house tomorrow, but she must also agree."

"About how much do you think you will want for it?" I asked.

"For me, nearly nothing, but she must decide that too." She handed Neil the keys. "Please excuse the state of the place. I haven't cleaned it for a long time."

"Bien, bien."

The house where Encarna and her sister had grown up was one of a row of three, sandwiched between old Matías's and a rather drab summer residence. On pushing open the stiff door I saw that the old tiled floor must have been mopped not so very long ago and there was only a little dust on the furniture – dark, solid stuff, similar to mine. María Jesús said she believed the house had last been reformed in the 1970s and had been occupied until only six or seven years ago, when Encarna's mother had died. Its distribution was similar to that of a British three-bedroomed terraced house and it had a biggish patio like mine, also overlooking a weedy field. As we toured the rooms Neil remained silent as María Jesús and I found minor faults like loose tiles, small patches of damp and cracks in the ceilings. On returning to the small hallway Neil stood there, frowning and scratching his shaven chin.

"Do you not like it?" I asked in Spanish.

He smiled wistfully. "I love it, but I don't want to get my hopes up," he murmured in English. "I like it, María Jesús."

"I'm glad."

"Yes, I like the house and where it is, near Jack's house." He pulled open the door. "I will go to speak to Encarna now."

She laid a hand on his arm. "No, don't go."

"Why not?"

"Because although you're wearing a serious expression, a child could tell that you like the house a lot. Encarna isn't a greedy woman, but I know her sister less well and she may be."

He nodded.

"Do you understand?" I asked.

"Sí, entiendo."

She smiled. "Allow me to speak to her first, Neil."

"All right, but I want to pay a… not too cheap price."

"A fair price, of course. I'll take the key back but I'll say nothing for now. Next week when I go to buy something I'll mention that you might be interested, if the price is right."

"Not too cheap, not too expensive."

She chuckled. "Precisely."

He smiled, then frowned. "Oh, maybe her sister not want to sell."

"Maybe not. Did you like the other house too?"

He smiled. "Yes, I think so."

"Then I'll ask Paco to contact the owner. I must go now. I'll see you both at the bar soon."

"Muchas gracias, María Jesús," said my eager friend.

"De nada. Jack, don't let him go to the shop for a while."

"I won't."

As we varnished the planks, Neil jabbered away about the house he hoped would soon be his.

"Oh, Jack, could you not feel the feng shui in there?"

"It felt all right. What's the feng shui like here?"

"Oh, great, great, but I really felt at home there. It reminded me of my childhood home a bit. It felt just right. I hope they'll sell it. It doesn't need so much work and I could do most of it myself. I mean, some people would throw pots of money at it, but I like it the way it is. I'd keep most of the furniture too, like you have. How much do you think it'll cost?"

"Fifty grand," I said off the top of my head, now amused by his fervour rather than alarmed as I had been at first.

"Yes, that sounds about right to me too."

"Really? My house cost less than that, you know, although it really did need doing up."

"I've studied the Spanish market and I think it's a fair price."

"Don't get your hopes up though. Try to put it out of your mind for now."

"I will. Two planks to go, then another coat tomorrow."

"Another?"

"Of course. We mustn't do things by halves."

We varnished for a while.

"You won't mind me living so close to you, will you, Jack?"

I sighed. "You might end up in that other house."

"No, I've a gut feeling that it won't be that one."

He was right about that, because when we entered the bar at about seven that evening Paco beckoned me into the kitchen.

"I called Bernardo in Altea," he murmured.

"Who? Oh, the man with the house?"

"Yes, and the old devil wants a hundred thousand for it. I told him he was mad and he said no, not mad, but he doesn't need the money and he prefers it to stand empty than sell it for less. He couldn't care less about the future of the village, of course. His family were always a mean lot."

"What's the place like inside?"

"Not too good. It needs work. Tell Neil to forget it." He cocked his ear and frowned. "And tell him right now not to mention Encarna's house. If word gets back to her that he's keen the price will go up."

As I stepped around the bar I saw Neil beaming down at Juanjo. As well as him, Toni, Miguel (Zaragoza) and Alfredo (Albacete), there were two more men I hadn't seen before. Summer really had arrived.

"Yes, the Encarna house is like my old house, so I–"

I slapped him on the back. "Shut your gob. Not a word about the house," I muttered. "Hola, Juanjo."

"Hola, Jack. Neil was saying something about a house, but I didn't quite understand."

I briefly mentioned the expensive one, but not Encarna's. "Oh, and I'm looking for a person to rent a room from you."

"Yes, Neil tried to tell me, and Paco explained it more clearly. A young Spanish person, he said."

"That's the idea."

"Not more foreigners?"

"Not for now, no."

"I fancied a Swedish divorcee of forty or fifty, but if that cannot be." He shrugged.

"It might be arranged one day, but not just yet."

"All right, I'll wait. Will I have to cook for this young Spanish person?"

"No, just let them use the kitchen when they need to." I had a thought. "Er, what's your house like?"

"When I bought it from my brother and sister I had Pablo do some work on it. If someone comes I'll clean it thoroughly."

"Ah, good."

"Neil told me that a pretty young woman is coming to stay with you soon."

"Yes, just for a visit."

"Would she not prefer to live in an authentic Spanish home rather than with you two?" he said with a sly smile.

I was dying to tell him that he really ought to clip the hairs in his nostrils and ears, but decided to leave that to his pal Neil. "Who knows? I'm sure you'll meet her, so she can decide."

He guffawed like the ingenuous soul he was, bless him.

"By the way, why do we never see women in here, except María Jesús?"

He shrugged. "The local ladies don't like it. The summer ladies sometimes come in."

"I see." I stretched and yawned. I wasn't sleepy, but the other blokes were making a hell of a racket, each talking over the other, about politics rather than football. "I'm off now. Are you staying for a while?" I asked Neil in Spanish.

"Sí, only for one hour, then I make dinner."

"Not a word about the house," I muttered.

"No, Jack."

14

The next day I was privileged to see Neil's luggage spread all over his room. As well as packing clothes for all seasons, he'd brought a good selection of hand tools, some bicycle parts, his drawing and watercolour painting gear, other sundry items, and about fifty books.

"May I?" I said, making a beeline for the box of books.

"Of course, but they're mostly crime stuff. I kept my favourites and took the rest to a charity shop."

"Wow," I said on seeing books by revered Crime Noir authors such as Dashiell Hammett, Raymond Chandler, Jim Thompson, James M. Cain and David Goodis, as well as True Crime classics by Truman Capote, James Ellroy, Ann Rule and Vincent Bugliosi. "This is a great collection, Neil."

He smiled. "Feel free to borrow them."

"Thanks, I… will." I'd been about to say that I'd read most of them and wouldn't mind reading some again, but remembered that I had yet to tell him I was a crime writer myself. "I can't see any British authors here."

He came over and peered into the half-empty box. "Hmm, here's a Dorothy Sayers, and there's a P. D. James in there somewhere, but I prefer the Americans on the whole. I like their hard-boiled style."

"No Agatha Christie?"

He screwed up his nose. "Not my cup of tea at all. Oh, there's an old book here that you might like." He took a slim cardboard package from a drawer in the wardrobe and pulled a bubble-wrapped book from it. He slid out the old volume with an ugly mottled cover and handed it to me.

I looked at the spine. "Oh, *A Study in Scarlet*, the first Sherlock Holmes book." I flicked through it. "Ha, with illustrations too. It must be a pretty old edition."

"It's a first edition."

"You're kidding?" I looked at the date, 1888, and closed it with care. "You're not kidding."

He smiled. "I inherited it."

"It must be worth thousands," I said, still gawping at that little piece of literary history.

"Oh, the really valuable book is the *Beaton's Christmas Annual* that the story first appeared in the year before, but this one, even without the paper cover, is probably worth about twenty thousand."

"And you brought it on your bike?"

"Ha, yes, I preferred that to the courier. My wife never knew its true value and I'm glad I didn't tell her now."

"So are you an expert in first editions?"

"No, only this one." He shrugged. "My great-great-grandfather was lucky enough to pick it up on a trip to London. He was a wool merchant."

"A Yorkshireman?"

"Oh, aye."

"Will you sell it one day?"

"One day, if I need to, but I'd like to leave it to Brad, though he's not much of a reader."

I touched the cover. "You shouldn't leave it in bubble wrap, you know. I think old books are supposed to breathe."

We then spent about ten minutes deciding where best to keep it and concluded that between other books on a wardrobe shelf was probably the best bet.

"And pop another book on top to keep the dust off," I said.

"Yes, I will."

"Would you like to read the book I'm writing? It's only a first draft, but I'd like to know what you think of it."

He smiled. "Of course, I'd love to. What's it about?"

"It's a cri– … well, just read it and see what you think." His book collection had made me realise that he ought to be a good judge of crime novels but, daft as it may sound, it was his fortuitous ownership of a classic book that had tipped the balance. "What are you reading now, Neil?"

"Oh, I've got some modern books on my tablet, but I always go back to the old ones when I fancy a really good read." He looked at the mess around him. "I'll sort this out a bit, then varnish the shelves again."

"I'll make a start now."

Over the coming days we worked like Trojans, first putting up the shelves in the study, then rendering the patio walls. It was while hosing the end wall one morning to prevent the new cement from drying too quickly that Neil told me he'd finished reading my manuscript. He hadn't said a word about it until then and I wasn't even sure that he'd started it.

I chuckled nervously. "What do you think of it?"

He shut off the hose, laid it down and wiped the sweat from his tanned, rather noble brow. "It's... well, do you want me to be straight with you?"

I pictured a future of poverty, taking in half a dozen lodgers to make ends meet. "Er, yes, please."

He nibbled his bottom lip and nodded. "Well, first of all I think it's very accomplished."

I sighed with relief.

"It's a very good book and I think it's the sort of thing people will enjoy. It kept me turning the pages and the ending was quite a surprise. Do you have a publisher for it?"

"Yes," I said, before telling him that I'd already published two quirky flops and two more conventional crime novels. "The detective in the story is appearing for the second time."

"Yes, I guessed that, and I think you should use him again."

"Oh, good. Would you like to read the first book he's in?"

"Yes, I would. Yes, he's a convincing sleuth, but, well..."

Fearing that he was about to dismiss all my suspects as two-dimensional cut-out characters, I was mightily relieved when he singled out only one of them, a... well, it doesn't matter who, but he suggested that I read through her participation in the story and then try to subtly reduce her presence.

"Oh, OK. Why's that?"

"Because she leads you to expect more from her, then she just fades away. She isn't, er… consistent." He shrugged and put his hands on his hips. "I may be wrong, of course, as I'm no writer, after all."

"No, but it's readers who read my books, not writers. Thanks, Neil. When I go back to it I'll see what I can do with her."

"Yes, just see what you think." He cleared his throat. "Then there's that scene in the working men's club."

"Ah, yes. What about it?"

"Well, I mean, have you spent much time in those places?"

"Not really. I remember going to one with my dad in Hawick years ago, but that's all."

"Well, they might be different in Scotland, I don't know, but I've spent a bit of time in them and… well, if you like we could read through the scene and I'll just point out a couple of things that didn't quite ring true. Just details, you know, but you might as well get them right."

"Yes, we can do that, thanks."

He nodded and turned on the hose, before turning it off again. "Just one more thing."

I chuckled. "The last?"

"Yes, the last. It's about the murder scene."

Me being a one-corpse crime writer, I knew the one he meant. "What about it?"

"He shouldn't twist the knife."

"No? I thought that was a nice sadistic touch."

He shook his head. "At the time I thought it was all right, but when I found out who did it I thought, no, he wouldn't have twisted the knife, not him. You might be accused of misleading the reader, because the twisting will make some of them rule him out as a suspect. Just a nice hard stab would be better, in my opinion."

"OK, I'll change that bit too." All these suggested revisions made me want to open the laptop and start sorting it out right away, but I contented myself with noting down Neil's suggestions and fetching him a hardback copy of my last book.

"This is for you, Neil. It's the last one I wrote."

He beamed and wiped his hands on his old shorts. "Oh, thanks, Jack. Can you sign it for me?"

Being a veteran of precisely four book signings, all sedate affairs, it was the work of an instant to inscribe a line of gratitude and sign my pen name with a flourish. I then added my real signature in the bottom corner to make it unique among the thousands... well, dozens of books I'd signed.

"Oh, thank you, Jack. I'll treasure this."

I laughed. "Put it alongside *A Study in Scarlet*. It might bring me luck."

His eyes sparkled but his face remained serious. "Who knows what the future may bring, Jack. You're still quite young, after all."

"Yes, and I want to write something different after this one."

He nodded and went back to his hosing.

In the second box, unceremoniously shoved under a travel iron and other bits and bobs, I'd spotted Neil's Spanish language books, so that evening, instead of going to the bar for our usual pre-dinner aperitifs, we adjourned to the patio to get to grips with his wayward grammar. We concentrated on the verb conjugations in the different tenses and I saw that he'd studied them, but needed to commit them to memory more thoroughly.

"When you speak you don't have time to think, which is why you make mistakes."

"Yes, I reckon that's it. That and the fact that I try to speak too fast."

"You ought to type out some sheets with the most important verb conjugations. You can borrow my spare laptop, if you like, and use my printer."

He nodded. "All right, thanks, I'll do that."

"Then keep them somewhere handy. Ha, last winter I typed out three sheets and kept them in the bathroom, so that when I sat on the bog I could go through them."

He smiled. "I could stick them on my bathroom door. I'll be able to read them from the loo."

"Good idea."

"Oh, but it won't be just my bathroom for long, as Jenny will soon be here. She might not like that."

I chuckled. "Or she might be grateful for them. She only got a Spanish GCSE, after all, and that was about… fifteen years ago, I guess."

"I'm looking forward to meeting her."

"Yes, me too, though I hope she won't disturb our, er… harmonious arrangement."

He smiled. "We are getting on well, aren't we, Jack?"

"Yes."

"To tell you the truth I thought you'd find me more of a pain in the arse. Linda found me dull and repetitive, she told me before she left."

"That was nice of her." I handed him the grammar book I'd been preaching from and stood up. "No, there's plenty of room for the two of us here, and I must say I enjoy your company. I was... well, I got bored sometimes before you came."

"Hmm, I'll be sad to leave in some ways, but of course I'll only be three doors away."

I wagged my finger at him, almost touching his beaky nose. "Don't get your hopes up about Encarna's house. We haven't heard from María Jesús yet, so there might be nothing doing."

"No news is good news, I hope. I'm sure she'll have spoken to her about it, so Encarna's probably already talked to her sister, so they're probably deciding how much to ask for it, don't you think, Jack?"

I raised two crossed fingers and went inside to prepare the dinner.

15

Two days later Neil finally went for a ride on his bike, which still lived in the study, as apart from two decrepit easy chairs, a shaky table, an ancient standard lamp varnished by him, and our beautiful, empty shelves, there wasn't much else in there. He rode about fifty miles and over dinner told me in no uncertain terms that it had been simply marvellous.

"Oh, Jack, you ride for miles without seeing a single car. It's a cyclists' paradise. I got as far as a tidy little place called Tragacete, then turned round. Oh, it was so wild on that road. I only went through two little villages the whole way."

"Was the road not rough?"

"Rough? Compared to the lanes in Yorkshire it was like a motorway. Oh, to think of the traffic I had to put up with to get anywhere nice from Castleford. It was a lot easier without the luggage and I don't think I've enjoyed a ride so much for years. I mean, I'm not even that keen a cyclist."

"No? You certainly sound like one."

"Oh, my old club mates would *love* it here. The roads, the hills, the scenery, and no flaming cars to spoil it. You know, I bet cycling holidays here would be really popular."

"Yes, I've seen a few people pottering around on mountain bikes."

He flapped his hand dismissively. "No, I mean real cyclists, but of course they could mountain bike on the tracks too. I tell you, Jack, it's a cyclists' paradise. I got within about forty miles of Cuenca. Maybe we could go there one day."

"Yes, I want to get some garden furniture before… soon, though I doubt it'll fit in the car. Maybe I'd get some in Molina."

"Oh, buy some online from Ikea or somewhere like that."

"I prefer to shop locally."

"Yes, but you can't be paying double the price for everything you want, can you?"

"No, Neil, I can't," I said, as my book sales had fallen again that month, as they usually do until I bring a new one out.

"I thought you Scots were meant to be thrifty anyway."

"I try to be. I'll have a look online later."

When we drove to Cuenca the next day we saw the sights – the hanging houses, the bridge over the ravine, etc. – before visiting the hypermarket to do our shopping and order four tasteful wooden garden chairs and a matching table. We then went to a nearby garden centre and Neil selected a few hardy shrubs and plants for the patio, him being an inveterate gardener as well as a DIY expert.

"I'm glad I won't have a garden at my new house. She made me spend hours in ours, but didn't do much herself. Why do husbands always end up doing most of the gardening, Jack?"

"In Glasgow we just had some plants and a window box on the terrace. She looked after them," I said, wondering if Nicola was spending much time there or if she'd already moved in with the doctor.

On the drive back it rained for only the third time since I'd arrived in the village. For the last half hour it really threw it down and made the landscape look drab and rather forbidding.

"I wouldn't like to be stuck outside in this, Jack."

"No, it all seems very different. I can see now why it was a tough place to live in the old days. Imagine traipsing home from the fields in this after a hard day's toil. I guess it'll be quite grim here in winter when the sun's not shining."

He rubbed his hands together. "I'm looking forward to some proper snow though, like we used to get when I was a lad. I'll get that wood-burning stove going and make the house cosy."

"The village sometimes gets cut off, Paco told me."

"I know, it'll be great, won't it?"

"Well, for a short time it might, yes."

"Great writing weather, I imagine. No distractions, you know."

"Yes. Yes, and I'll be writing a more serious book next winter, I think."

"Hmm."

I glanced over, but he was looking out of his window. "I don't just want to write crime stories all my life."

He looked through the windscreen. "But that's your forte, I think."

I chuckled. "Hmm, but I might have another forte if only I give it a go. Jenny appears to be a serious writer. She's had short stories published in some good magazines."

"Yes." He looked at me. "Yes, you could write a couple of stories and see if they'll publish them. Then you'll know if you're on the right track. Ooh, look, blue sky up ahead."

When we got back the sun was steaming the moisture off the streets and our brief taste of things to come was over. We found a note from María Jesús on the doormat, asking Neil to pop round to the bar, so after he'd helped me to bring in the plants he scampered off. I carried them through to the patio, watered all six of them, had a shower, and reached the bar at about seven. When I spotted a bottle of cava on the counter and saw Neil's arms flailing around, I suspected that he'd had some good news. I opened the door and steeled myself.

"Jack! Encarna's going to sell me the house," he boomed in English, a language we tried not to speak in the presence of our neighbours.

"Muy bien," I said. Only Paco and Juanjo were present.

Paco filled a glass and handed it to me. "Your friend is a hasty fool, Jack. Drink this now as I want to finish it before the others arrive." He shook his large head. "What a way to go about things."

I knocked back the fizzy stuff. Paco refilled our glasses and dumped the bottle into the bin.

"What's happened?" I asked Neil in Spanish.

"Well, Encarna tell María Jesús that they sell, so I call her and say yes."

Paco whipped Juanjo's empty glass from under his nose and placed it out of sight. I gathered that he found the consumption of cava on his premises somewhat distasteful, so I emptied mine and handed it to him.

"Encarna asked sixty thousand for the house," Paco explained. "So this *tonto* here simply agreed, although even a child knows that sixty means fifty."

"I don't care," Neil said in Spanish. "Maybe someone else buy if I… wait."

"Oh, yes," said Paco. "There would have been a long line of people queueing down the street, all waving banknotes." He shook his head. "One doesn't go about things in this way. Neil, give me that glass right now. The others mustn't know what a fool you've been."

I slapped Neil on the back and congratulated him.

"Gracias, Jack. I think it is a fair price. Pablo is going to do work on the roof before I buy, Encarna says."

When the others arrived we all had bottles of beer and Paco deftly steered the subject from the house purchase to agricultural matters. When María Jesús appeared in the kitchen and beckoned to me, I steered Neil around the bar and she took us up and over to their sitting room.

"So, Jack, what do you think about Neil buying the house?" she said when she'd seated us on the sofa with our beers.

"I'm glad. He really wanted it, so it's great news. Don't you think he should have haggled though?"

She shrugged. "He wouldn't have gained much, as Encarna isn't stupid. She's fixing the roof too, which will be cheaper for her, as Pablo's her cousin. It's better to have goodwill, I think, than to save a little money. He can use her lawyer to do the paperwork too, so it will be quite straightforward. Far better than buying from that miser who lives in Alicante."

I agreed that he'd done the right thing, but wondered if he'd have agreed to the price with such alacrity if she'd asked seventy or even eighty thousand.

"So, Neil, can you pay for the house right away?" I asked him.

"Yes, I have money enough, just."

"Good. Tell María Jesús about your first edition."

He told her about his copy of *Estudio en Escarlata*, getting the Spanish name right first time.

"Oh, my goodness, what a rare book that must be," said the bibliophile who had hundreds of books along the wall furthest from the stove. "You must show it to me, Neil, but don't tell people how valuable it is."

I chuckled. "Do you ever have burglaries here? Paco told me there was no crime in the village."

"Not by the villagers, no. When I was a girl one poor man stole two hens to eat, but he was caught right away and had to pay for them. The main danger is from strangers who are passing through. Only last year two hooded men tried to rob the petrol station at Beteta. One carried a long knife."

"What happened?"

"Well, the attendant wasn't used to things like that happening around here."

"Do they hurt him?" Neil asked.

"Or tie him up?"

She smiled. "No, he just knocked the knife from the man's hand with a lump of wood and they ran away, only to be caught later. Those men were Spanish, but there is talk of foreign gangs who travel around committing robberies." She tapped the table. "So far they haven't ventured here, but one must be aware of the danger. Before people hardly ever locked their doors, but now we always lock them at night."

"In my new house I make a good place put the book," Neil said, still beaming and paying little attention to his grammar.

I smiled. "What will I do without you, Neil?"

"Oh, it is some time before I go, Jack, and then we are still neighbours."

"It *will be* some time before I go, and then we *will* still be neighbours," I said, or words to that effect.

"Oh, Jack, I am too happy for grammar now."

"I'm happy too," said María Jesús. "First you, Jack, and now Neil. The village is already changing."

Neil nodded. "And soon Jenny, and then maybe a Spanish person."

"Yes, Jenny's arrival will be interesting," she said.

I remembered something. "Neil read my story and he says that he liked it."

"Oh, yes, a novel crime stupendous," he enthused.

I told her that he was something of an authority on the genre, so I was relieved that he'd approved. "And he made some good suggestions." I grinned. "I'll start to revise it soon."

"Please stay for dinner. It's good to see such enthusiastic people."

16

A few days before Jenny was due to arrive I began to revise my novel. I usually sense when the time is ripe to reassess my work and I was loath to put it off until after she'd settled in. I also wanted this aspiring literary author to see me on the job from the word go. She might not think much of the kind of books I wrote, but at least she'd see that I applied myself to my craft and would hopefully get on with her book too. Besides, although she'd seemed ever so agreeable during our call, I thought it wise to establish a solemn landlord-lodger relationship at first, as there'd be time enough for friendship to develop if we saw that we hit it off.

You might think I'd be eager to pursue a romantic liaison with the charming young lady, but nothing was further from my mind. Although the failure of my marriage with Nicola had hit me hard, I was too proud to seek a quick fix by trying to work my magic, such as it was, on Jenny. I was, or would be, on the rebound and I vowed to steer clear of eligible females for a while longer. Mixed in with this stoical stance there was also the fear of rejection, of course, but the upshot was that I meant to behave like the perfect Scottish gentleman – polite, considerate and even a trifle distant, like a laird in exile from his loch-side castle.

Five days later, when she called from Cuenca to say that she'd missed the bus to Beteta and would have to spend the night there, I told her not to talk such nonsense and that I'd be there within an hour and a half.

"But it's miles away, Jack, and you told me I'd have to make my own way there."

I forced myself not to smile. "Yes, well, I've finished my work for the day and I quite fancy a drive in the country."

"I really don't mind staying here, you know, although I have got rather a lot of luggage."

I grinned, then clamped my teeth together. "Are you at the bus station?"

"Yes."

"I'll be there by six."

She chuckled. "Thanks, Jack, it's very kind of you."

"Bye for now, Jenny."

Neil had just gone off to the woods with his drawing pad, intending, he'd said, to try to get his old touch back, so I had no choice but to go alone.

After a brisk drive I arrived at the station in Cuenca at 5.47 and found her in the cafe, gazing at her tablet. I stood watching her for a while as she read and made notes in a tiny pad. She can't have been very photogenic, or telegenic, because she was even lovelier in the flesh. Her pale skin was flawless, her small nose exquisite and her big blue-grey eyes like I imagined those of Athena – the Greek goddess of poetry, among other things – to be. She was slim, but not boyishly so, and had refined hands and cute little feet. I remember she wore a light-blue t-shirt, cream-coloured slacks and brown sandals, but of course us writers train ourselves to be observant.

I approached before she caught me gawping at her. "Hello, Jenny."

"Ah, hello, Jack." She stood up and offered me her hand, which I grasped as softly as if it were a cream cake. "I'm so grateful you've come."

I shrugged and pointed at her pad on the table. "Working?"

"Yes, just going through a passage for the twentieth time. I can't seem to get it right," she said in her mellifluous voice.

"Is it the novel you said you were writing?"

"Yes, and I'm finding it hard work. It isn't at all like writing short stories." She stowed the tablet and notepad in the top pocket of the large rucksack which stood beside a big suitcase. "Would you like a drink before we go?"

"No, thanks, unless you do."

She giggled. "I've had three coffees already."

(An aside: When I say that she giggled, I don't mean she giggled like a giddy girl, but that whereas many people chuckle, she giggled instead. It was her way of expressing amusement, and a very charming way too.)

"You've brought quite a lot of luggage."

"Well, I was going to come for a fortnight, but in the end I decided to bring enough for a longer stay. You both seemed so nice when we spoke that I felt sure I'd want to spend the summer here, if that's all right with you, that is."

I nodded gravely, having managed not to grin inanely so far. "Oh, yes, we want people to stay for a while, hopefully with a view to, er… staying for longer."

"Yes, I know. I have to go to a literary festival in Salisbury in October, so I guess that'll be the time when I make a decision, unless you're fed up of me by then, of course."

"Oh, I doubt it."

"Are you sure you don't want a drink or something to eat, Jack? You seem a bit tired."

Not tired, just playing it cool, I thought. I smiled. "A quick coffee then, to perk me up."

She caught the waiter's attention with ease, before ordering my coffee and asking for the bill in a fairly good Spanish accent. When the time came to depart I insisted on carrying the heavy rucksack, as the suitcase had wheels.

She giggled. "I did manage to get it this far, you know."

I shouldered it with manful ease, though it was surprisingly heavy. "What have you got in here?"

"My laptop, clothes and books. I can't live without my books. I expect you've got lots of them."

"Yes, but still in Glasgow, alas." I'd long since removed my ring, but there was no avoiding the subject of my marriage. "My ex is looking after them for now. The car's this way."

After admiring my brown Suzuki Grand Vitara, which I'd quickly jet-washed on the outskirts of the city, I drove calmly through the rush-hour traffic and out into the countryside. The first part of the drive back was along a straight main road and she glanced into the back a couple of times.

"Do you need something?"

"Oh, I was going to grab my pad and pen, but it doesn't matter."

I pulled over in the next lay-by and allowed her to retrieve the tools of her trade, tools that I rarely carried unless I was out researching something specific. After scribbling a few short phrases she shut the pad and sighed contentedly.

"Ah, it's so good to be away from London at last. I loved it there at first, meeting all kinds of people through work and going to lots of parties, but I feel in dire need of a change of scene."

She was a good, concise talker rather than a natterer and had soon told me that after studying English literature at Durham University she'd initially secured an internship at the publishing house where she'd ended up staying until a week ago.

"They've been eight good years, but London wears you down eventually. What about you, Jack?"

I told her even more concisely about my studies in Edinburgh and my years of teaching in Glasgow, before finally confessing that I was a crime writer.

Rather than sniggering or spitting on the floor, she said how interesting that was and how that type of writing would be beyond her.

"Really?"

"Yes, I'm hopeless with plots."

"Oh, right. Do you not have, er… plots in your stories?"

She giggled. "Of a sort, I suppose, but my stories are more about people and situations than action. In the one I won a prize for hardly anything happens at all. My mother thought it was a bit pointless and was surprised the judges liked it, but I told her they were all steeped in modern stuff and that I'd tried to write something they'd like. A bit cynical, I suppose, but a prize is handy when it comes to offering a novel to a publisher. It's a snobbish world really and I think that hardly anything that the critics enthuse about now will still be read in twenty years' time. It's like a big literary whorehouse, if that's not putting it too crudely."

I chuckled. "I was short-listed for a crime novel prize once," I said, pleased by her frankness, as I too thought almost all modern literary authors overrated.

"That's handy too. No doubt my publishers, whoever they turn out to be, will put mine forward for some first novel prize or other." She snorted daintily. "I wish I could just write and publish and not have to jump through so many hoops, but that's the way it is."

"Hmm."

"That's why I have to go to Salisbury in October, to pick up my prize and try to rub shoulders with other authors and critics who might write me a good review when my book finally comes out. Then I'll return the favour, and so it goes on. Paulo Coelho called it the Favour Bank in one of his novels, and he was right. You scratch my back and I'll scratch yours is the way it goes, I'm afraid."

"I don't bother too much with that. Maybe I should."

"Tell me about your books."

I told her briefly about my two quirky flops, my two conventional novels and my work in progress. She asked me if my last one was selling well and I gave her some approximate figures.

"Oh, that's really good, Jack," she said, patting my bare arm and making the skin tingle. "If my book sells so well I'll be absolutely delighted."

"Well, I'm pleased with the sales, but if you think about it you have to write one a year to make a half-decent living."

"Ha, I've been working on mine for over a year and I've still got a long way to go."

"So how do literary authors get by?" I said, a question I'd often asked myself.

"Oh, they go to conferences, workshops and other events, and write reviews and articles." She laughed. "They spend more time doing that than writing their books. That's one reason I'd like to live somewhere quiet and cheap, so that I don't need to earn so much. Rent in London has always been dear, but now it's becoming ridiculous."

I smiled. "That's part of the reason I've come here too," I said, before I found myself telling her about the fortuitous nature of the house purchase and the subsequent disintegration of my relationship with Nicola. I couldn't believe I was being so frank, as although I had no designs on Jenny there was no need to confess that I'd been cuckolded, but I told her about the damn doctor too, fool that I am, although I refrained from mentioning why we went to see him.

She tutted sympathetically. "It might be all for the best."

"Yes, I hope so."

"Relationships can be complicated and unpredictable."

"Yes."

"One never knows where one really stands."

"No, I discovered that."

"When I found out that my boyfriend had been unfaithful I was distraught for a while."

I gulped. "Ah."

"I forgave him eventually, but I've told him that we must spend some time apart."

"Yes, good idea… I suppose."

"He'll want to come and see me, but I won't let him."

"No."

"And in October we'll see where we stand."

"Yes. Yes, hopefully by then you'll know what to do. Is he a writer too?"

"Yes, worse luck. You might have heard of him. He's called John Smith," she said, though that's a clever pseudonym I've thought wise to use.

"Oh, right, yes, I have heard of him. He's well thought of, isn't he?"

"Yes, especially by himself. He was long-listed for the Booker a few years ago and has dined out on it ever since. More than dined out, in fact, as I think that's what's kept him in print. He's a very… difficult author to read."

"Yes, I believe so. I've never tried, I'm afraid."

"The literary snobs like that, as they pretend to understand work that he doesn't really understand himself."

"Ha, I see."

"If you ask me, he's bogus."

"I see."

She giggled. "He's a fake, a charlatan and an opportunist."

"Right," I said, warming to the man.

She shrugged. "But I love the silly sod, worse luck, and even feel a bit sorry for him."

"Why's that? I think I saw him on telly once," I said rather foolishly.

"Oh, he's the biggest bum-licker in the business. He does anything to get a bit of attention. I feel sorry for him because it's all going to come crumbling down one day soon. He *is* bogus, you see, he's practically told me so himself, and you can't fool the people forever." She sighed. "And the worst thing is that he won't be able to handle it. He won't be able to accept that his time in the limelight is over and that he'll have to get a teaching job or something."

"Isn't he a bit older than you?"

"More than a bit. He's forty-six now."

"I'm thirty-nine," I said, tilting my chin up slightly. "I'll be forty next year," I added helpfully.

"Well, they do say life begins at forty."

"Yes, and I want to test that theory by writing something different, something... you know, more literary."

She pouted divinely and I resolved to keep my eyes on the road, as it was becoming more sinuous.

"You could do that, I suppose, but if you're becoming successful at what you're doing, I'm not sure you shouldn't stick at that for a while longer."

"Oh, I'll..." I was going to say 'knock off'. "...write another crime novel, but I'd like to try my hand at something more serious too."

"Write a couple of stories then."

"That's just what Neil said."

"Oh, please tell me about Neil. He seems ever so nice," she said, and that was the end of our literary banter for the time being, something that I'll try not to harp on about too much.

"Neil is… settling in, and he's about to buy a house. You'll meet him in half an hour. What do you think of the countryside?"

"Pleasant in the sun, but wild. It reminds me of Derbyshire in some ways, but without the drystone walls."

"Did you not fancy living there?"

"Too expensive, and I don't really want to live at home. I need peace and quiet to write."

"Me too," I said, before droning on about the depopulation of the area until we reached the village. "This is it."

"I like it. It's rustic and pretty, but not too pretty. Just the sort of place I yearned for when I was in London."

"Well, you're here now."

17

On pulling up in front of the house Neil came loping out, beaming from ear to ear, and proceeded to make a tremendous fuss over Jenny. This suited me fine, as we'd talked for two hours and it was about time I tried to resume the affable but slightly aloof posture that had lasted about three minutes. When he shouldered her rucksack *and* grasped the suitcase I loitered near the car until he'd ushered her inside, chattering away like a gangly public schoolboy welcoming a new boy to the house, save for his undiminished Yorkshire accent, of course.

The problem was that although Jenny and I had bonded remarkably well in so short a time, thanks in part to our common interest and her apparent respect for my crime writing, I already felt strongly attracted to her. This wouldn't do, I told myself as I wiped the dead insects from the windscreen. If she perceived this threat to her tranquillity she might hop it after a fortnight and I'd soon find myself alone in the house, as I imagined Encarna would allow Neil to begin to settle in before the paperwork was completed, though she might not. Despite my initial reservations, I'd got used to hearing the patter of size eleven feet around the place and enjoyed the time we spent together, so, all things considered, resuming my sole occupancy wasn't what I desired.

I looked at my reflection in the rear window with the intention of trying out a couple of reticent expressions, but found myself admiring the taut, tanned skin of my pleasant though rather ordinary face. I didn't look a day over… thirty-seven, I told myself, and although John Smith, author and poseur extraordinaire, was a handsome chap, he was starting to show the effects of so many cocktail parties. Realising that I was thinking the wrong kind of thoughts, I slapped my cheeks and groaned, unaware that Jenny was on the doorstep.

"What's up, Jack?"

"Oh, a mosquito. We don't get many, but they have a nasty bite." I locked the car. "I'll show you your room."

"Neil's already shown me. I like it."

"Good. Oh, we'll have to get you a desk."

She chuckled. "Neil's looking into it right now. He's suggested ordering one from Ikea or somewhere like that and is trying to get online."

"The internet's a bit temperamental here, though it does work most of the time."

"I won't need it much, and the phone even less." She sighed and closed her eyes, enjoying the cooling breeze. Her short hair suited her and she reminded me a bit of Jane Fonda in her younger days, although Jenny's face was more refined. "I'll answer any important emails, but apart from that I want no connection with the outside world for a while."

"I expect you'll want to have a shower now."

"Yes, Neil told me I was to use the downstairs bathroom."

"Did he? How odd. No, the one upstairs is new and more convenient for you. I'll leave you some towels and then make something for dinner."

She chuckled. "Neil says he's going to make chicken and oven chips."

"We aren't very good cooks, I'm afraid."

"I'm not too bad."

"We'll go shopping in Molina soon." I shuffled my feet and scratched my neck. "I'll go and find you some towels."

"Thanks, Jack."

I found Neil in his sitting room, cursing my spare laptop.

"What's up, Neil?"

"Oh, I can't get this thing to work and we must get Jenny a desk. I showed her the bedroom and her face fell when she saw there was no table at all. I told her she could work in here or in the study and she agreed, but I could tell she was disappointed. Damn this thing. If I can order one now it might arrive in two days."

I snorted. "Don't make such a fuss over her, Neil. It's up to her to get a desk if she really wants one. We aren't her nannies, after all," I said somewhat harshly.

He smiled. "You did go to pick her up though, didn't you?"

I shrugged and looked out of the window. "Well, you know, a young woman alone in a strange city."

He laughed. "She's lovely, isn't she?"

"She's all right."

"She's like a breath of fresh air, Jack. I don't know about you, but I mean to enjoy my time here with her, without disturbing her at work, of course." He prodded a couple of keys. "And for that she needs a desk."

I turned from the window. "And who's going to pay for it?" I muttered.

He looked up calmly and shrugged. "I will. A desk is a handy bit of kit and I don't mind buying you one. I'm living here cheaply enough anyway. Is something the matter, Jack?"

I strode over to the door and closed it, before pacing up and down, scratching my head. "Nothing's the matter, but I want to keep my distance," I said, finally sitting down opposite him and quietly expounding my fears.

He listened patiently, nodding and chewing his lip.

"… and in the end I'll spoil everything and drive her away."

He chuckled softly. "Oh, Jack, she'll be used to it by now."

"Used to what?"

"To men drooling over her. Even in London she must have stood out from the crowd, and hobnobbing with literary folk she'll have had more propositions than soft Mick."

"She's seeing that writer, John Smith."

"Never heard of him. Look, just be yourself, Jack, and everything will be fine. If you pretend not to like her you'll just make yourself look daft. I'd better go and switch the oven on."

"Is chicken and oven chips the best we can do?"

He smiled. "We shouldn't make a fuss over her. Besides, she might as well find out right away that we're not much cop in the kitchen."

When he'd left I prodded a few keys on the laptop and smiled. After connecting to the Wi-Fi I located a decent desk on a furniture website. I thought about asking Jenny if she liked it, but decided just to buy it. It would be mine anyway, and when she'd gone back to her pillock of a boyfriend I might well use it myself.

Neil's sensible words must have done the trick, because over dinner I felt like my old, unemotional self once more. We talked about the village and villagers, Neil's new house, our half-hearted quest for a Spanish lodger and whatever else occurred to us. Jenny was a good listener and only spoke about herself when asked, usually briefly.

"Will you be working tomorrow?" I asked her when her eyes had begun to droop.

"I'd like to do two or three hours in the morning, if that's all right."

"I'll be revising in the morning too."

"And I'll keep out of your way," said Neil. "My drawing is coming along and I'll be off up to the woods early doors. Ha, one day I might be able to illustrate one of your books."

I remembered his Sherlock Holmes first edition and smiled. "Novels aren't normally illustrated these days."

Jenny patted my arm. "Who knows what you'll write in the future, Jack. Well, thanks ever so much for being so kind. I really must turn in now."

Neil leapt up and held open the already open door. "Buenas noches, Jenny, and sleep well," he said in Spanish.

"Gracias. I will see you in the morning. Buenas noches."

"Buenas noches."

Neil closed the door softly behind her. "Her Spanish seems OK."

"Yes, it does."

"Feeling better now?"

I yawned. "Yes, I think so."

"I'll do the washing up. You get yourself off to bed. You have brainwork to do in the morning."

I stood up. "Thanks, Neil."

"And don't go into the wrong room, eh?"

"No, Neil."

After shaving and inspecting my face for signs of ageing, I composed myself for sleep in a better frame of mind. Jenny was the first attractive woman I'd found myself in close quarters with since leaving Glasgow, but I'd soon get used to having her around. The fact that she was in the room next to mine and would be sharing my bathroom didn't trouble me in the least. It would be a new experience to share a house with another writer and perhaps fate had sent her along to help me unlock the literary genius I felt sure was lurking somewhere inside me. Yes, that was sure to happen, I thought as I drifted off to sleep.

18

In order to set a good example I got up at seven o'clock the next morning, made a jug of filter coffee and took a cup into my sitting room, where I set about diligently revising the third chapter of my book. The good thing about revising is that you can knock off whenever you want. It's advisable to take frequent breaks, in fact, so that you don't start speeding ahead instead of scrutinising every sentence carefully, so when I heard Jenny and Neil pottering around in the kitchen I decided to join them. I'd only been working for half an hour, but I'd been concentrating awfully hard.

"Oh, Jack, we didn't disturb you, did we?" Neil said in a hushed voice.

I laughed. "Course not. Did you sleep well, Jenny?"

"Yes, thanks, it's a nice hard bed."

"Yes, I... believe so."

"Well, I'm going to finish my weetabix and leave you two geniuses to it," he said, indicating his drawing pad on the spare chair.

"May I?" said Jenny, who looked lovelier than ever in the morning light. She wore no make-up that I could discern and nor had she the previous day. It would have been wasted on her.

"Of course, feel free."

We both agreed that Neil's drawings of the nearby woods and rocky outcrops were very promising.

He shrugged. "Oh, I'm still out of practice. I told you a little fib in my email, Jack, as I hadn't drawn or painted for years, but you said you wanted creative people and… well, now that I've started again I'm really glad. I could have gone to the Bradford School of Art, you know, but ended up being a postman instead." He sighed. "I was too keen to earn money, I suppose."

"You're only fifty-five though," I said.

"Fifty-six, but yes, I'm not so old."

"Monet was a late starter and painted his best pictures when he was older than you," Jenny said. "I saw some of them in the National Gallery."

"Really? Ooh, I feel keener already. I hope I really take to it, because it's important to have something creative to do. You've got your writing, which must be really rewarding, and I don't think going cycling and doing up my house will be enough to keep me occupied, especially my mind, which I must keep active," he babbled, which was fine by me, as I could observe Jenny's expressions of assent, wonderment and well-veiled amusement. I'd never put a truly attractive woman in any of my novels and maybe I'd use her as a model someday.

The trio of artists soon went their separate ways, Jenny choosing to work at the table in their sitting room, only a few yards from where I sat at mine. I could access the kitchen directly, so when I went for more coffee an hour later I thought it only polite to take the jug into her room and offer her a drop. The door was ajar, so I tapped and pushed it open.

"Hi, Jack. Oh, thanks, I'd love some."

I filled her cup and glanced at her laptop screen. "Is it going well?"

"Not really. I'm still working on the same passage as yesterday. I just can't seem to get it right."

I chuckled and leant on the table. "If I get stuck like that I just move on and come back to it later. Ha, I usually find that it wasn't so bad after all, but then again I'm only writing for… well, a less fussy readership," I said, narrowly avoiding saying something more disparaging about the people who paid my bills.

"Yes, maybe I should do that." She closed the lid and gazed up at me, so I backed off an inch or two. "The trouble is that I'm used to writing stories about twelve pages long. I know the people who read them are looking for a clever turn of phrase more than anything else, so I polish them up, over and over again, even though the first version said basically the same thing." She sighed and ran her fingers through her glossy brown hair. "Do you have any suggestions, Jack?"

"Me? Well, I… I… have you plotted out the story?"

"Oh, God, yes, down to the last detail. Look at this." She handed me a large notebook. On leafing through it I saw page after page of small, neat handwriting, interspersed with little flow charts and other baffling diagrams.

"You've gone into a lot of detail," I said, weighing it in my hand.

"I know, I know. As I'm so bad at plots I thought I'd better make sure I had one from the word go. John helped me with it a bit, though he wanted both of the main characters to commit suicide together at the end and I can't possibly do that. I mean, I'm not setting out to depress the pants off people, after all."

"No, dual suicides are a bit over the top."

"How do you go about planning a novel, Jack?"

I promised you I wouldn't overdo the literary chitchat, so although we talked for another hour I'll try to be succinct. I told her that when I started writing a novel I usually had up to half a dozen vaguely defined characters, a place or places where the action was to take place, and a flexible plot idea. I basically made it up as I went along and often found that the most unexpected things happened, even more so since I'd speeded up. One character might usurp another, or I'd find myself in Belfast rather than Bristol, or an antique musket would be replaced by an old Scottish dirk – a long dagger – as had occurred in my work in progress. Having an established detective had made my latest effort a little more circumscribed, I told her, but the rest of the cast had ended up acting of their own accord, if that didn't sound too pretentious.

"Not at all. I believe many great authors wrote like that. I'd really like to read your last novel, Jack."

"Hang on, I'll see if I can find one."

I went to fetch one from the pile of nine I had in a cupboard and handed it to her.

"Thank you, Jack. The cover's very good."

"Yes, my publisher chose it... though I approved it, of course. Ha, I hope you like what's inside as much. For anyone used to reading serious books it'll seem very simply written, but one has to give the public what it wants." I shrugged. "In the past I've written what I thought were really good descriptions of landscape and things, but ended up having to cut them out. That's why I want to test myself more after this one." My eyes met hers and I smiled shyly. "That's where you could give me some good advice, I think, if you're still here then."

She smiled back, more candidly. "I'm not intending to go any time soon, Jack. Now that I've met you both in the flesh and seen how kind you are and how lovely the house and village are, you might find it hard to get rid of me."

I then performed a whistling laugh, or laughing whistle, but whatever it was it sounded absurd. I cleared my throat to prevent further strange vocal emanations. "Ha, there's plenty of room here for all of us, or both of us once Neil has moved out."

"Mm, could you sign the book for me, Jack."

"Of course, er... what shall I write?"

She giggled. "Whatever you like."

"Oh, I... er... I'll have to think about it." I grasped the small volume. "I'll leave you to it now." I made for the door.

"Jack?"

"Yes?"

"I won't be able to read the book if you take it with you."

"Ha, no, how silly of me." I returned it to the table. "See you in a while then."

"All right. In about an hour I think I'll go for a walk."

"Right, yes, the best place to go is up the street, then along the lane… though I could come with you, unless you prefer to go alone."

She smiled yet again. "No, I'd rather you came with me. If we're lucky we might catch Neil in the act."

"Eh? I mean, sorry?"

"Drawing."

"Ah, yes."

During the next hour I got very little work done, as every time I focused on the screen Jenny's face smiled back at me. By the time we set off it was already getting quite hot, so I asked her if she'd applied plenty of sun cream to her pale, slender arms and slim but well-defined legs, though not in those exact words. She assured me she had, so I led the way along the empty street and up the lane towards where I thought Neil would be drawing. A bolder man would have avoided the spot, but her buoyant stride and the way she kept turning to smile at me was reducing me to a tongue-tied wretch, so I was eager to have the aspiring artist entertain her for a while.

Then something extremely surprising happened. On approaching a pine-scented glade I instinctively threw back my hand and caught Jenny in the midriff, not because I could stand her presence no longer, but because I'd spotted a couple canoodling under a tree. She saw them too and suppressed a giggle, before we backtracked and headed off along another rough path.

"They seemed a little old for that sort of thing, especially him, though I don't suppose he's much older than Neil," she said when we'd covered some ground.

"Two years older," I said, before informing her that the ageing Romeo was my friend Juanjo, the confirmed bachelor.

"And who was she?"

"I didn't see her very well, but I hope she's one of the summer women."

"Why?"

"Well, as far as I know there are no unattached women in the village between the ages of twenty and sixty, and if she's a married village woman he could be playing with fire, literally, as all the men have shotguns here," I said, subconsciously hoping that she'd cling to me in fear, but she just giggled.

"But if she's one of the summer women, she'll probably be married too, won't she?"

"That's true, but the husband may not be here yet."

"And when he comes he won't bring his gun."

"Probably not, though he might have one in the house." I shook my head and smiled. "I'd never have though it of Juanjo. I mean, I know he likes the ladies, but I thought it was all talk. He's a dark horse all right."

"A rather grizzled horse, I thought, but they seemed to be getting down to it."

As we were then in another glade, I shuffled back a bit, lest she think I fancied a roll on the pine needles too, which I did, but I preferred her not to sense it.

"Ha, if you ever write about the village, you'll have to put this bit in," she said. "Mysterious romance in the woods, ageing bachelor and unknown female, then keep the reader hanging on for a while."

"Or you could write about the village, Jenny."

"Oh, I probably won't be… I don't know, part of me wants to start a whole new life and leave London behind forever, but I suspect I'll feel the pull of civilisation after a while." Her silky-smooth brow wrinkled a little. "I'd love to be like D.H. Lawrence, always moving on to new and exotic places, but I doubt I'll be so adventurous."

"Then there's John Smith, of course."

She scowled prettily. "God knows what he'll be up now I'm no longer around. I'd rather not talk about him, Jack, if you don't mind."

"Not another word. Come on, we might find Neil over towards those little cliffs."

We soon saw him up ahead, sitting on a rock with his pad perched on his legs.

"Should we tell him about our discovery?" she murmured.

"Oh… no, we'd better not just yet. He chats to the men in the bar a lot, you see, and him being a bit guileless he might put his foot in it."

"Is Neil guileless?"

"Well, he gives me that impression."

"Hmm, I'm not so sure," she whispered. "Hola, Neil!" she cried.

He looked around and beamed. "Ah, there you are." He pushed himself to his feet and offered Jenny his comfortable rock. "Isn't it a lovely day?" With his green peaked cap set jauntily on his head he looked like a perennial boy scout out earning his thousandth badge.

I wiped my forehead. "Yes, but it's getting a bit hot now."

"After smelly London and damp Derbyshire it's wonderful," said Jenny, her skin untainted by a single drop of sweat.

After admiring Neil's drawing, a slightly superior version of the scene he'd already shown us, we set off back to the village.

"Can we go to the bar for a drink?" she asked as we approached the house.

I chuckled. "You don't have to ask."

Neil coughed politely. "Yes, but... er, I think you should change first, Jenny, dear."

(Jenny, dear? I couldn't imagine plucking up the courage to call her that, unless we ever... but no, and Neil was old enough to be her father, after all.)

"Really?" she said.

"Being a Sunday the bar will be full of blokes at this time, but you don't *have* to change," I said, not being an old fuddy-duddy like my pal.

"I'll put on some slacks and a more decent top then. I don't want to look *too* much like a tourist."

19

The bar was fuller than I'd ever seen it, as practically every local patron and quite a few summer men were there, all yelling to make themselves heard. The din lessened momentarily when they saw Jenny, and Toni gallantly vacated his stool for her, but they soon resumed their football and politics chatter. I ordered three beers and introduced my new lodger to Paco.

"Welcome to the village, Jenny," he yelled slowly. "My wife is looking forward to meeting you. Jack, would you like to take her through to the house now?"

"Did you get that?" I said to her.

"Yes, but I'll stay here for a bit."

I looked at Paco and span a forefinger horizontally to indicate 'later'. He nodded and flicked the tops off a few more bottles.

I told Jenny that he only really made any money in summer and that he kept the bar open in order to keep the village alive.

"Paco's a grand chap," said Neil. "And here's another grand chap," he added, beckoning Juanjo over to our little enclave.

"Buenos días," he said, clean-shaven for once and looking flushed in a long-sleeved checked shirt which I examined for sylvan debris but found none. "You must be Jenny."

"Sí, pleased to meet you, Juanjo."

"Ah, you already know my name," he said, before planting two firm kisses on her cheeks, which became immediately rosier due to her minor slip, unless it was just his animal presence.

"Sí, because Jack and Neil told me a lot about you," she said slowly and correctly in a passable accent.

"Ah, I see. Well, I think these two bachelors need a good woman to look after them."

She giggled. "No, they have to look after me."

"What have you been up to this morning, Juanjo?" I asked.

"Oh, after feeding my pigs and chickens I took a stroll in the woods with my shotgun."

"With your shotgun?" I leant towards Jenny and murmured, "A good metaphor," causing her to cover her mouth and narrow her eyes.

"Yes, to see if I could shoot a rabbit or two, but I found none. I've never been lucky as a hunter. I think I tread too heavily."

I resisted an impulse to pursue an innuendo-infused interrogation in order to amuse Jenny, mainly because Neil wasn't in on the secret. I said that I was still looking for a Spanish lodger for him.

"Ah, yes, I wished to speak to you about that, Jack." He sipped his beer, smacked his lips and ruffled his already ruffled hair. "After giving it some more thought, I'm not sure if it's such a good idea after all."

I glanced at Jenny and she nodded.

"Why's that, Juanjo?" I asked.

"We-ell (in Spanish: bue-eno), I've realised that I'm fairly stuck in my ways after living alone for so long, and having a young person to stay might not be so good for me, or for them, as I'm not the tidiest man in the world. My sister, when she visits, says that I keep my pigsty cleaner than the house so, all things considered, I'd rather not have a lodger for now."

I looked at Jenny and she shook her head. "He's getting cold feet about the lodger I'm supposed to be finding him. I wonder if this morning has anything to do with it," I said rapidly. "Er, Juanjo, and if the prospective lodger were a woman, would that make you reconsider?"

He smiled, then shook his head. "I'm afraid not. I fear that a woman would like my house even less than a man. Sorry, Jack, but right now I can't take a lodger."

Jenny indicated that she'd understood, so I asked him if he might change his mind after the summer.

He sipped his beer, was about to speak, then took another sip. The cogs were turning and needed lubrication. "Well, right now I don't think so, Jack, but when the cooler weather arrives I may feel more inclined to give the house a really good clean. It's also lonelier here in winter, so I might want some company, so… well, I'll let you know after the summer."

Jenny nodded.

"Yes, I suppose you have plenty of company right now," I said.

He began to make a sweeping motion but almost spilt a man's wine. "Perdón, Tomás. Yes, as you can see, there are plenty of men for me to talk to now. Summer is a lively time here."

During this conversation Jenny and I had exchanged a few knowing looks, so when we left the bar Neil wanted to know what we were up to.

"Oh, I'd told Jenny that I was sure Juanjo was getting cold feet about the lodger project and that I meant to put him on the spot."

"Hmm." He stroked his cheeks. "I don't think you're allowed to hunt rabbits now, but I may be mistaken."

"Oh, we're supposed to be seeing María Jesús," I said, stopping outside the house door. "Do you feel like meeting her now, Jenny?"

"Is she the cultured lady you told me about?"

"Yes."

"I'd like to meet her then."

María Jesús is a marvel in the kitchen and insisted on rustling up a few things for lunch. Despite being a monoglot, her grasp of language is so good that from the word go I'd understood practically everything she said, so even when she began to talk about literature Jenny was able to understand her. Although a GCSE isn't much, she'd followed it up with further studies and several trips to Spain, so at that time she spoke more correctly than Neil but had a less extensive vocabulary. I was ahead of them both, but not by all that much, so I vowed to carry on swotting, listening and chatting whenever I could.

We also talked about Neil's future house and he said that he was in no great hurry to move. Encarna had already offered him a set of keys so that he could get on with some work, he said, but he preferred to wait until nearer the time of the sale.

"I thought you would be eager to start doing things," I said in Spanish.

"Sí y no. When I start I not want to stop and it is still long time before house mine. It is better I wait a little. Also now is summer, time to relax and enjoy, so better I start in… five, six weeks, I think."

I was wondering if Jenny's arrival had influenced his decision when María Jesús interrupted my train of thought with some news that I didn't find as welcome as I might have done a fortnight earlier.

"My cousin in Madrid knows a young man who may wish to come to live in the village for a time," she said.

"Oh, good," said Neil.

Jenny smiled.

"Ah," I said. "Who, er… is he?"

She chuckled. "Her son. He has finished his master's degree, he cannot find work, and he doesn't wish to go to do some menial job in a foreign city," she said clearly, checking that we'd all understood.

Neil beamed at us. "Tell him to come to visit right away."

"Wait. Juanjo doesn't want a lodger now," I said.

"Ah, yes, I forgot."

A pregnant silence ensued, as the ball was clearly in my court.

"Tell us more about him, María Jesús."

"Well, I haven't seen him for a long time, but I remember him being a quiet, studious boy."

Is he as ugly as sin? I wanted to ask. "How old is he now?" I did ask.

"Twenty-five or six. He studied philosophy, so of course it's practically impossible for him to find a job, as they employ few philosophy teachers nowadays."

"Hmm, we need practical people here really. I mean, what would he do, educate the men in the bar about Plato and Aristotle?" I said in a jovial attempt to dispel the slight tension caused by the negative vibes I must have been emanating.

She smiled. "I believe he's especially keen on *estoicismo* now, or so his mother tells me."

Neil mouthed the unfamiliar word. "Ah, stoicism, as in being stoical," he said in English. "Well that is the better philosophy for living in a place like this, no?"

María Jesús moved her head from side to side. "In theory, yes, but his mother thinks it would be more stoical of him to go to England or Germany to earn some money, as some of his friends are doing."

"Yes, he should do that," I said. "For a while anyway. It would be a good experience for him."

Jenny looked over and her soft blue eyes prevented me from firmly vetoing the philosopher's entry into my realm, whose population I had no wish to increase just then.

"Going abroad isn't for everybody, Jack, and he should have an opportunity to do something here, in his own country," she said.

"Of course."

"Village like this need young people," said Neil. "This is what we are saying for weeks, no?"

Occasionally when I'm writing I come up with a cunning plan to get a character out of a tight spot and one occurred to me now. I bestowed a charming smile on one and all.

"Well, as Neil is about to reform his house, this lad..."

"Jaime."

"Jaime could help him with that. Then he would learn valuable building skills which would be useful for him in these difficult times."

Jenny nodded thoughtfully.

Neil copied María Jesús's non-committal side-to-side cranial manoeuvre.

Our hostess tittered.

"What?" I said.

"As a boy he was very clumsy. The other children would do sport or play on the little playground that the provincial council later dismantled because it became too dangerous. Jaime usually sat nearby, reading a comic or a book, partly because his coordination was so poor. That may have helped to make him a fine student, but I don't think he'll be very good at practical tasks."

Two escape clauses occurred to me.

"So do his family still have a house here?" was the first.

"No, they sold it about ten years ago." She shrugged. "Yet another family lost to the village."

"A local boy should be able to return to his village," said Jenny.

"But if he can't *do* anything, what will he… do here?" was the second.

They just gazed at me, but as luck would have it Paco chose that moment to come thudding down the stairs. He was a practical man and would no doubt back me up in my campaign to avoid taking in a lodger who appeared to be neither creative nor capable of useful manual work.

He slumped onto a chair at the end of the table. "Oh, it's been so busy in there today. I thought they'd never go home for lunch."

His wife brought him a plate and cutlery.

"Have you closed now?" Jenny asked.

"I cannot close. No sooner has the last man gone home for lunch than the first comes for coffee. Juanjo is in charge now. I'll take him some food in a while."

"He seems happy today," I said, glancing at Jenny.

"Happy? Juanjo is always happy. I've never known such an optimistic man, despite his life being quite monotonous."

Neil caught me smirking at Jenny and raised his eyebrows.

"Paco, what do you think about Jaime coming to stay?" I said.

"Jaime? Ah, yes, young Jaime." He stabbed a bit of squid and chewed it thoughtfully. "He can stay with Juanjo."

"He just told us he no longer wants a lodger. Did you not hear?"

"One can't hear a thing in there when they're all shouting. That's strange. Only a few days ago he was saying how eager he was for you to find him someone. He told me he'd cleaned his house from top to bottom."

"Well, that is *very* strange," said Neil.

I kicked him under the table and frowned.

"What's strange, Neil?" said María Jesús.

"Oh, nothing," he said, a little confused.

"Jaime could come to my house," I said quickly. "But only if he has something... constructive to do." All eyes were upon me. "I mean, if he wants to visit for a week and needs somewhere to stay, that's fine, but if he wishes to stay for longer he must have some kind of... er, mission. Jenny and I have our writing and Neil has his art and will soon be working on his house, so whoever comes must... well, what do you all think?"

"He could come to visit for a week," said Jenny.

"Yes," said Neil absently.

I shrugged. "I don't mind that."

Paco waved his fork. "Jaime appears to be a capable young man. His father told me that at university he became involved in student campaigns about... I can't remember what now."

"The oppressive measures of the government at the time," María Jesús said. "Yes, I'd forgotten about that. I believe he was quite active in Madrid and was almost arrested once."

"So he is not only a philosopher then," said Jenny.

"Hmm, perhaps he would be a useful person to help to attract more people to the village," said Paco. "He is in touch with young city folk, after all, and may be able to persuade some of them to come here."

I pictured my house turning into a student commune, with all-night debates, dope smoking, free love and general anarchy. "I still think that people who come here must be creative or have practical skills."

María Jesús smiled at me. "Look, I'll invite him here for a few days, then you can meet him."

"That's a good idea," said Jenny.

Neil was still ruminating about the kick under the table.

"I prefer that. Then we can talk and see if a longer stay at my house is a good idea," I said.

"I'll call him soon. So, Jenny, please tell me more about your writing..."

As soon as we left the house Neil bent to rub his shin.

"Sorry about that, Neil. It was to do with Juanjo. I'll tell you when we get home."

Neil was amused and a little shocked to hear about Juanjo's tryst in the woods.

Jenny giggled. "It's not so surprising, Neil. He's only a little older than you, after all."

"I know, and I certainly don't feel past it. I still hope to meet someone someday, but I doubt I'd... court her in the woods."

We debated Juanjo's possible motives for his open-air romance and concluded that his lover must be a summer woman whose husband wouldn't arrive until August.

"She's probably an old flame and their love has rekindled after many years," Jenny said.

"Yes, but she seemed younger than him, judging by her slim body," I said.

"María Jesús is also slim," she said.

"That's true."

Neil gasped. "You don't think it was her, do you?"

I laughed. "No, and her hair was browner. I wonder what this Jaime will be like."

"You don't seem too keen on him coming," said Neil.

I shrugged. "I'd got used to the idea of Juanjo taking in the next lodger," I said, but later on I had to admit to myself that Jenny's arrival was to blame for my change of heart. I reminded myself of the loathsome John Smith and her probable desire to return to city life and told myself to snap out of it. There was nothing doing, so the best thing I could do was to treat her no differently from Neil. She was a friendly lodger, and nothing more.

20

My friendly lodgers and I soon got into a pleasant routine of work or art in the morning, lunch at home, longish siestas, and social life in the evening, either among ourselves on the patio or at the bar, where Paco had illegally placed a few tables outside, but no-one pulled the popular mayor up about this minor transgression. This outdoor option made the bar more amenable to some of the summer women, and we couldn't help trying to identify Juanjo's lover, with little success, as it was hard to picture any of the demure ladies frolicking with him in the woods. Jenny's easy manner made her just as well-liked as Neil, and I think I was seen as the least forthcoming of the three foreigners, although I tried my best to be chatty.

One day we drove into Molina to do our shopping and for Neil to open a bank account, something that Jenny didn't feel the need for just yet, although she seemed to be thoroughly enjoying her time with us. By dint of masterly self-control I believe I managed to come across as a great platonic pal, although if anything my feelings for her deepened, especially after she gave me her opinion of my work. I was just about to knock off after a gruelling morning's revision when she tapped on my door – which almost always remained ajar when I was on the job – and breezed in with my last book.

"Jack, I'm very angry with you," she said with a charming mock-angry expression on her lightly tanned face, her being far too refined to allow her skin to turn purple as Neil's had done after many drawing sessions and a few bike rides. My tan was a sort of pinky-brown, by the way, and not too bad for a Scot.

I cringed on seeing the book. "Don't tell me, it was so bad that it's affected your ability to write good prose."

"No, but I found it so gripping that I simply had to finish it this morning when I should have been working on a tiresome description that's turning my hair grey."

I looked at her hair like a concerned older brother. "Not yet."

"Even the lovely desk that you and Neil put together for me couldn't stop me from sneaking off to the sofa to read the last couple of chapters."

"I see," I said, suspecting that she was exaggerating a bit, as several days had passed since I'd given her the 270-page book. "Did you not find it a little shallow though?"

Her unplucked brows rose exquisitely. "Shallow?"

"Well, you know, very simply written."

She frowned. "Many great writers wrote simply. Most of the truly great ones, in fact. I'm trying to cut down on the flowery prose myself, as I want normal people to read my novel, not just competition judges, critics and… other pseuds. I don't read many crime novels, but yours has shown me that straightforward writing can be quite deep."

I sniggered and kneaded my brow, wondering if it was the equivalent of April Fools' Day in Spain. (They celebrate *Holy Innocents' Day* on 28th December, I found out later.)

"I'm not joking, Jack. Your detective and the woman who I was convinced was the murderer but wasn't are great characters. The plot is marvellous too. It's a really good book."

I blushed becomingly. "Thanks."

"Would you let me read the one you're working on now?"

"Yes, of course. Neil's read the first draft and given me some advice. When I get to the end of this revision I'll be printing it out anyway. How's your story going?"

She shook her head. "Slowly, too slowly. I've been thinking about what you said about having to write a book a year to make a go of it and at this rate I'll be on bread and cheese before long."

I lowered my bushy brows from which I'd plucked a couple of grey hairs that very morning. "Er, don't worry too much about the rent, by the way. We are fellow writers, after all."

"Oh, I'm joking. I have quite a bit saved and I'll be fine for a year or two, but what then?"

Marry me and write as slowly as you want, I thought, before recalling that I was still married and only a chum.

I smiled. "I'm sure your novel will be a success, Jenny, then the publisher will be crying out for another one."

"I hope so."

"Apart from being distracted by my pot-boiler, are you finding it easy to work here?"

"Oh, yes. In London I had to have classical music on softly all the time because of the street noise, but here it's so quiet that I even look forward to hearing people walk past." She smiled. "It reminds me of where I am and how much I like it here." She reached both hands in the air and stretched, so I lowered my gaze. "Come and sit down for a bit."

On my way to the sofa, which I'd sat upon with her before with no ill effects, I thought the time was ripe for us writers to discuss a certain matter. I sat down at one end and she at the other, facing me with her feet on the middle cushion. I felt a strong urge to stroke those petite feet, but instead reminded her that Jaime was due to arrive at his aunt and uncle's house in three days' time.

"Yes, I know. I'm looking forward to meeting him."

"Me too, but I'm still… concerned about him coming to stay here."

She smiled. "I know. This project to attract people to the village is ever such a good idea, but of course you don't *have* to invite him here."

"Oh, I'd like to, but I'm concerned about you."

"Me? But I'm all for it."

I pointed at the wall and jabbed my finger. "That is effectively your writing room. If someone else comes they'll have to be able to sit and relax somewhere, and I'm not going to let them use this room, I'm afraid."

She chuckled. "But the three of us often spend time here."

"That's different. You're my friends."

She laughed. "But the idea is for Jaime to join our happy group. He'll make us speak more Spanish. You know, I think you've got preconceived ideas about him and they aren't positive ones. I wonder why that is."

I shrugged, unable to unburden my soul. "I'm really thinking about our working time. You have your haven and you mustn't be disturbed."

"Oh, but we could easily carry the desk into the study, or to my bedroom for that matter. There's a good view from the back of the house. Yes, I'll do that if he comes to stay."

Damn and blast the size of this house, I thought.

"It won't be so long before Neil begins to move out anyway. It'll seem very quiet here without him. What's the matter?" she said, as I'd just stifled a fiendish grin.

"Neil's all for this lodger project. If anything he's keener than me about it."

"Yes, he seems to be."

"He'll soon be a house owner, with two spare rooms."

"That's true."

"And he'll need some help there. Even if this Jaime is as clumsy as they say, he'll still be able to carry things and mix cement and whatnot."

"Yes, unless he has other plans. He might need peace and quiet like we do."

I smiled. "He might, but I'll speak to Neil about it anyway."

She grasped her ankles and pulled her feet closer to her body. "You know, Jack, if I didn't know you better I'd say that you wanted to keep me all to yourself," she said with a mischievous glint in her eyes.

"Ha, course not." I stood up. "I'd better finish what I was doing."

"Yes, me too. Oh, please sign your book for me."

I found a good pen and wrote:

For Jenny, a future star in the literary firmament. Best wishes, and added my pen name, before scribbling my real signature in the corner so that Sotheby's would one day have two priceless editions of my breakthrough novel to auction.

"Thanks a lot, Jack." She giggled. "But you haven't even read any of my stories yet."

"I was waiting for you to ask me to."

"I was waiting for *you* to ask."

"Would you like me to read what you're writing now?"

"Oh, no, I don't think I could handle any criticism at this point. When I finish the first draft I'll probably ask you to read it, then I guess I'll start all over again."

My idea of a thorough revision is to change a sentence here and there and occasionally remove or insert a paragraph, but I knew that literary authors often completely rewrote their books several times. Hemingway claimed to have written forty-seven different endings to *A Farewell to Arms*, and on reading his final choice I couldn't help thinking that the third, sixteenth, or thirty-ninth version would have been just as good, but I'm not a big fan of the bearded braggart.

"Why would you start all over again, Jenny?"

She shrugged. "Most people do. John does. He changes everything around and it becomes even more confusing, or complex, as his friendly critics put it."

I adopted what I imagined to be a Byronesque pose and gazed out of the window. "Let me read it first before you do anything like that. I find that one normally writes what one wishes to write the first time around. Dickens and Tolstoy wrote their great works against the clock, because they were initially published a chapter at a time in newspapers. All these flashbacks that modern authors use are nothing but gimmicks, if you ask me."

"You used a couple in you book."

"Did I? Oh, yes, I remember now. I thought them… expedient."

She smiled. "They worked anyway. I'll print out one of my better stories for you later. I'll really value your opinion, you being a successful author already."

I shrugged and looked away. "In a very modest way."

She stood up. "Oh, when are we going to paint the patio walls with that nice pastel paint you bought?"

"We could… wait a bit, as Neil tells me that moisture remains in the cement for a long time," I said, though I was sure it was as dry as a bone by then. I shoved that task up my metaphorical sleeve, where I'd already stored a couple more, just in case.

"Of course I'll be delighted to host young Jaime, once I'm installed," Neil said that evening on the patio after watering the plants. "But Encarna says the notary will be on holiday until the end of August, so it'll be over a month until the house is officially mine." He rubbed his neck. "It'll be too hot to do much work until then anyway. Yes, I'll have plenty of time to put my house in order once the summer visitors have gone. It'll seem very quiet here then."

"I'll be sad to see them go," said Jenny.

This was good news, as it suggested she had no thoughts of leaving. Her trip to the literary festival in Salisbury was still over two months away, but I knew that would be decision time for her. Would she finally rid herself of the dastardly John Smith? I'd found a short video on YouTube of him harping on with two other trendy writers at some poorly attended conference and I was able to confirm my suspicions that he really was a first class twit with a balding head, dissipated face and the most insincere smile since Queen Elizabeth told her Scottish cousin Mary that she was more than welcome to holiday in England for as long as she wished. What on earth did Jenny see in that sallow, skinny jackass? Maybe in October, after spending so long among rational, pleasant, healthy folk – like me – she'd finally see the light and scurry back to Spain to spend the winter, where we'd while away the evenings snuggled up on the sofa before the wood-burning stove in my sitting room and…

"Won't you, Jack?"

"Eh?"

"Won't you be sorry to see the summer people go?"

"Oh, yes, in a way, but nothing concentrates the mind like…" I'd been about to say solitude, but that wouldn't do. "…being with a like-minded friend, or two."

"Yes, Jack," she said, smiling wryly as she made for the house.

21

On Friday María Jesús invited us for lunch to meet young Jaime, who was to stay for the weekend before dashing back to Madrid to attend a job interview. It was the hottest day of the summer so far – my thermometer in the shade reached thirty-six degrees – and we were relieved to enter their air-conditioned house just before two. María Jesús told us to make ourselves comfortable before returning to the kitchen area, where a powerful extractor fan prevented all but a hint of the delicious fishy food she was preparing from reaching us.

"Can I help?" said Jenny.

"There's nothing to do just now, dear. Paco's gone to Beteta to pick up Jaime. They won't be long. Open a couple of beers for the boys, if you like."

This she did, neither of them being radical feminists, before pouring white wine for herself and María Jesús, who was looking very lithe in a beige blouse and brown slacks under her apron. She was fifty-eight, like Juanjo, about whose affair we were yet to discover a thing.

"Is Juanjo looking after the bar now?" I asked.

"No, Toni's there. We haven't seen Juanjo since yesterday morning, which is unusual."

Jenny and I exchanged furtive glances, but Neil proceeded to astonish us both.

"María Jesús, does Juanjo have a woman friend at the moment?"

She chuckled as she stirred. "Yes, I believe so. Paco tells me he's become very friendly with Veronica, a woman who has lived in Valencia for many years. She has three teenage children and comes back to her house every summer."

"With her husband?" I asked.

She stopped stirring and gaped at me. "But of course not, God forbid. She was divorced about three years ago."

"Ah, I see. Is she an old school friend of Juanjo's?" I asked, the floodgates of my curiosity having burst open.

She chuckled. "Well, when Juanjo was leaving school she may have begun, but I don't think they were exactly friends. She's about fifty, I think."

Neil's beer appeared to have gone down the wrong way, but he was in fact spluttering with laughter. He patted his chest and coughed. "Oh, María Jesús, these two young people see Juanjo and friend in the woods and since that day they are thinking, who is it, who is it? They think it is big scandal and big secret, ho, ho."

"You too, Neil," I snapped.

"Yes, me too, until I think, this is not good, I will ask him, so I ask him, and he tell me."

Ignoring that fact that he appeared to have ignored my grammatical advice, I asked him why he hadn't told us.

"I tell you now. I was waiting for next time you and Jenny look one at other like bad children when we are with Juanjo." He slapped his thighs. "So, there is no scandal and everything is fine."

Jenny said she was glad.

I just nodded, struck dumb by my pal's forthright approach to a problem which, had it existed, might have disturbed the peace of the village, while Jenny and I had treated it merely as a bit of a joke.

"Did you know they were... so close?" I finally asked María Jesús.

She strolled over with her wine. "I suspected there was something between them, but I think they're trying to keep it a secret."

Neil raised a forefinger imperiously. "Yes, and we must not speak about it with other people. Juanjo says please not to."

"Why not?" Jenny asked.

"Well, he hopes to spend time in Valencia with her after the summer and he thinks that any gossip can be bad for this plan."

"What? The village can't afford to lose Juanjo," I wailed. "He is an... institution."

Neil shook his head. "Oh no, not lose him. Veronica's younger boy is seventeen. When he goes to study, maybe she comes back here." He beamed. "Very good news, no?"

"Excellent news," said María Jesús. "When... how did you find this out? I don't think even Paco knows."

"Oh, one evening we are talking outside the bar and I say let's take a stroll. We went to the square and he tell me there."

I chuckled. "You should have been a…. an investigative journalist, Neil."

He shrugged. "When I think my friends may have a problem, I must try to help."

Just then the front door flew open and Paco stomped in, followed by a tubby, unprepossessing young man with a clean-shaven, homely face and a short, sensible haircut. He wore a navy-blue t-shirt which displayed his flabby arms to good effect, smart blue jeans and clean brown shoes. He was all I'd feared he wouldn't be and I greeted him warmly. When he replied shyly with a quiet, 'Encantado, Jack,' and placed his soft damp hand in mine I could easily see him occupying the spare bedroom; a discreet, innocuous figure who would stick around until he got bored to death, then pack up and return to Madrid. That's what I thought then, I remember wistfully as I pen his entry into our lives.

After Jaime had been introduced to Jenny and Neil, who welcomed him affectionately, we sat down at the table and Paco brought over the large seafood paella. He began to eat straight from the pan, and while the rest of us served ourselves María Jesús asked after Jaime's mother and other family members. He answered briefly in his clear, quiet voice, after which he showed little inclination to address the three foreigners with whom he allegedly wished to live for a time.

"What kind of job is the interview for, Jaime?" I asked him.

He emptied his mouth of the half dozen grains of rice he'd forked into it, before patting his full lips with his napkin and clearing his throat. "It's for an administrative post in a telecommunications company."

"Oh, that sounds all right," said María Jesús, who he'd addressed as Aunt, though I guess they were really cousins once removed.

He shrugged his narrow shoulders. "It would be an acceptable job for now, but I have little chance of success. I have been to similar interviews and not been successful. I think the interviewers wish one to express great enthusiasm and... dynamism, but I merely state that I feel myself more than capable of doing such a straightforward job." He shrugged and patted his lips. "I refuse to play-act on these occasions. If they wish to employ a competent and reliable worker, they can offer me the job, but I will not pretend to be someone I am not," he said in a soporifically monotonous way.

I glanced at Jenny and Neil and they both nodded.

"But Jaime," Paco boomed. "You must play the game, son. Tell the *gilipollas* (wankers) what they want to hear and walk out of there with a job."

"I do try, Uncle, but I find it hard to be insincere."

"Well that is a good quality, Jaime," said the eternal optimist. (Not me, but Neil.)

"At some interviews they will like sincerity," said Jenny.

"Serve yourself some more, Jaime," said María Jesús.

"You'll never get a damn job like that, son," said Paco. "In this world you have to fight to get anywhere."

"Yes, Uncle, but..." He sliced off a piece of fish the size of a euro coin and nibbled it with his small but impeccable incisors while we waited. "In this world many people fight but are simply crushed by our consumer society. Take me, for example." He speared another little sliver of fish and I noticed that Neil's eyes were open wide and his mouth hanging slightly ajar. Jenny was chewing but alert. María Jesús smiled patiently. Paco shovelled from pan to mouth.

Jaime patted his lips again. "I was encouraged to study philosophy because my logical mind fitted me for such a pursuit. I studied diligently for five years and was then urged to continue my studies with a view to becoming a university teacher or at least a secondary school teacher. I was the best student on my master's course. I then wished to study for a doctorate, but the funding had ceased." He turned his placid gaze from the paella pan to Paco, who had stopped shovelling. "Uncle, you know that my parents cannot afford to finance such an undertaking, so I have no choice but to find work. There are no school-teaching posts whatsoever." He patted his lips. "I don't lament my choices, but I do feel somewhat cheated. I will go to the interview on Tuesday and do my best. One must be stoical, which often means resigning oneself to one's fate."

I'd half expected Paco to reply in his usual blustery way, but he just chewed and nodded.

"You may be lucky this time," said Jenny with a lovely smile which I'd rather she'd reserved for me.

He smiled back in a rather saintly way and his brown eyes sparkled slightly. "I hope so."

At this point, dear reader, I didn't know what the hell to make of this dull, flabby lad who had somehow transfixed or maybe even mesmerised us all with his monotonous but strangely intense voice. There was certainly more to him than initially met the eye, but I still wondered why the dickens he wished to stay with us in the village. Suspecting that María Jesús might have suggested the move to his mother and that he'd simply agreed out of politeness, I took a leaf out of Neil's book and asked him directly why he wanted to come to stay with us.

He took a tiny sip of wine, nodded slowly, then patted his lips. "I didn't, not at first anyway. My aunt told my mother that some foreigners had a house here and wished to attract young people to the village. She suggested that I might like to spend the summer here and I asked her how on earth I was going to find the job that she was so eager for me to get in the village." He made to pat his mouth, but desisted, perhaps feeling that he'd overdone that method of punctuating his sentences.

He fixed his gaze on me instead. "I called my aunt here to please my mother and it was only when she told me that your objective was not simply to provide summer accommodation and make some money, but to actively prevent the depopulation of this area that I became interested. I looked into the issue and soon found myself reading every article I could find online, before studying the state of affairs in other places too. The situation seems to be the same in many southern European countries and none of the governments are doing much about it, but then in our so-called democracies they never do address the malign effects of capitalism." He popped a prawn into his mouth and chewed for a while, before smiling in that beatific way of his. "So, I have become interested in your initiative and wish to lend a hand insofar as I am able."

"How will you do that?" I asked, as he'd directed his monologue mainly at me.

"Oh, I have several ideas which I will explain more fully after lunch."

"Yes, we all seem to have stopped eating," said his aunt. "Come on, tuck in before it goes cold."

A few mouthfuls later Neil said, "I am also buying a house in the village, Jaime."

"Encarna's place," Paco said.

"I will have two extra rooms and will also invite people to stay."

"Spaniards or foreigners?" he asked.

"Spaniards, I think."

"Good. Foreigners may bring wealth to the area, which is good, but Spaniards must come if we are to begin to tackle the fundamental problem of depopulation," he droned.

"Jaime, how is your sister enjoying married life?" María Jesús asked him. He took the hint and conversation became general until the table had been cleared.

In the meantime I mulled over what Jaime had said so far and tried to anticipate the threat to my sovereignty which I feared his proposals would pose. I'd deduced that he was an Ideas Man, and as such I didn't mind having him about the place. Our Spanish would improve as we sat around having cosy chats about depopulation, repopulation and related issues, and we'd all feel virtuous about our interest in rural affairs, but, and it was a big but, what if he backed up his words with actions and I suddenly found my house full of enthusiastic young people? All the bedrooms were quite big and once Neil had moved out, Jaime would dispose of his and another to further his – I mean our – aims. By installing bunk beds we could probably cram half a dozen more activists into the place and turn it into a veritable hotbed of radical repopulators.

I was having one of my catastrophist moments, of course, but by the time coffee was served I'd formulated my defence strategy, just in case. One body per room was to be my policy, which meant Jaime now and perhaps one more person after Neil had left. Each individual, furthermore, must have something constructive to do, and as Jaime was clearly a theorist, any further lodger would have to be more hands on and actually perform some kind of work. I stirred in a single cube of sugar and braced myself.

"What are your ideas for attracting people to the village?" Jenny asked him.

"I will tell you," he said, before fetching a folder from his bag, extracting some neatly printed sheets and putting on a pair of narrow reading glasses. I thought for a moment that he was going to hand the sheets around, but he instead studied the top one, now able to prod the bridge of his glasses instead of patting his mouth.

"These are just a few rough notes I made yesterday in an attempt to summarise the conclusions I have reached so far, but I am of course open to other ideas."

That's nice of you, I thought.

Paco began to fidget.

María Jesús looked mildly amused.

Jenny and Neil gazed at him attentively, in order to understand his droning, I hoped, as I'd find it hard to cope with three fanatics.

He prodded his glasses. "Task number one, which will occur at the same time as task number two, is to announce our project to the world. For this we will make use of the internet."

"Jack is already using that tweeter thing," said Paco.

"Twitter, but not very much," I said, as I hadn't repeated my post since Jenny had arrived, though nor had I removed it.

"I will personally design a website dedicated to our campaign. This I will begin right away, with your input, of course. Once it is active, *then* we will use social media to attract people to it. Random tweets and suchlike are of no use whatsoever."

"I come here because of a tweet," said Neil.

"Me too," said Jenny.

"I'll show you the tweet I use later," I said.

He pursed his lips and prodded his glasses. "Task number two, to find suitable accommodation for the new arrivals." He gazed at me and I steeled myself. He smiled. "It's kind of Jack to offer the use of his house. I for one am grateful. However, we must bear in mind that he is a writer, and so is Jenny."

I sighed silently. Was I off the hook already? Were Jenny and I to be left in peace to write and become great friends, until she gave John Smith his marching orders and our relationship could finally blossom?

Prod. "Because of their literary work, the house must be a quiet place, so I think that once Neil has moved to his own house, that room should be occupied by one tranquil person, or perhaps a couple."

"Er, a couple would mean five people in the house, Jaime," I said. "And Jenny and I really do need silence all day long in order to do our work."

"I'm not a noisy person."

"No."

"And nor would the couple be." Prod. "A couple would be especially beneficial, particularly if they were in a position to reproduce right away, as the village urgently requires children."

I chuckled, though it came out more like a sob. "Er, babies can be quite noisy, Jaime."

He smiled and shook his head. "Yes, but by the time of its birth the couple would have been rehoused." He then looked at Jenny and emitted a strange, strangled titter. "If you will permit me a not entirely serious suggestion, Jenny, it would be a good thing if you found yourself an unattached man from the village and, er... procreated with him."

She smiled. "I already have a partner, Jaime."

"Here, in... Spain?"

"No, there, in... England."

I kneaded my temples to hide my knitted brows. Was the podgy little lump trying to ascertain whether Jenny and I were an item? Did he intend to procreate with her himself? Dream on, foolish boy, I thought, and lowered my hand.

"Jaime, several young women from the village are now staying for the summer," María Jesús said with an encouraging smile. "Two or three of them are studying at university. You ought to meet them while you're here."

He blushed, so he must have had blood in his veins after all. "Yes, if I have time. So, continuing with my second point, it's essential for us to secure accommodation with local people here. I'll be busy with the website, so who will take responsibility for this task?"

Neil's hand shot up. "Me."

Jaime smiled patiently and took off his glasses. "Thank you, Neil, but unfortunately your Spanish is not yet good enough to persuade these... straightforward people to accommodate visitors." He looked at Paco and María Jesús. "Aunt, Uncle, I hope that you'll be willing to carry out this essential task, as you know everybody here."

She smiled indulgently, as if he were a child asking for a third helping of ice-cream. "I can certainly mention it to those I know well, Jaime, but I can't put pressure on my neighbours to host people they haven't met."

He nodded, seeming a bit miffed. "And you, Uncle?"

Paco shrugged, poured a drop of brandy into his coffee, then shrugged again. "For the last few years I've been aware that the village needs new blood. I bought the bar in order to keep this place alive and I open it all year round. When Jack arrived I finally saw some light at the end of the tunnel. When he agreed to take a lodger or two that light brightened, then Neil came and soon bought a house. Now Jenny is here. She likes it and, God willing, she will stay. In a short time more has been accomplished than in the last fifty years. The summer people see our new friends here and I think their perceptions have already begun to shift. At least one of my summer customers who was thinking of selling a house that his family no longer use now wishes to keep it." He shrugged. "Maybe now he will rent it to new arrivals, but my point is that Rome wasn't built in a day and we ought to do things little by little. This year our friends from England..."

"And Scotland," I said.

"And Scotland. Next year maybe some Spanish folk. There's no need to hurry so much."

And there I'd been, thinking he was half asleep.

"Thank you, Uncle." He put on his glasses and referred to his notes. "Task number three also involves you."

Paco grunted.

"As the mayor of the village, I wonder if you'll be able to secure some funding for our project. If I outline our proposals in a document, would you be able to submit it to the authorities?"

"Yes, I can do that, no problem."

"Ah, good, then I will draw up the document before I start on the website."

"But they won't give us a cent. I can't even get them to install a couple of litter bins, let alone resurface the main street with those pretty cobbles like they did in Beteta and a few other villages before the government cuts. No, anything we do here will be on our own initiative."

I coughed lightly, having just remembered something. "Er, the rent I've received from Neil and Jenny is for the project, so if you need some for the website, or anything else, just tell me, Jaime."

He nodded gravely. "Thank you, Jack. Yes, we must have a fund for expenses." He scribbled some notes. "We'll talk about that later. Task number four pertains to employment. Uncle, are there any jobs on offer here at the moment?"

"Not at the moment, no."

"Oh."

"As far as I recall, the last time a full-time, permanent job was offered here was when I created it myself, several years ago. I advertised for a shepherd and general helper. None of the few working people in the village was available and no-one from outside applied."

"So what did you do?" I asked.

He shrugged. "What I'd always done, get my friends to help me, as I helped them when required. The position I offered was an attempt to bring somebody new here. I thought that maybe some youngest from Molina would prefer to try working on the land rather than going to the city or abroad to work in a restaurant or something, but none applied. Now my son is in charge and he has no interest in bringing new people. He wants to leave, in fact, due to the lack of a school."

"I think people who come here must have something to do," I said more loudly than I'd intended, this being a pet subject of mine. "There is no work here, so they must have an occupation which they can do here."

"Yes, I..." Jaime began, but I'd hardly got into my stride.

"On this website you must make it clear that there are no jobs here. They must have an occupation. We think creative people might wish to come; writers, painters, sculptors and suchlike. Also people who can work online. If people come who have nothing to do it will be a waste of time, no use at all, just… dreaming."

Everybody except Jaime nodded at least once. He referred to his notes.

"Task... point number five, culture."

"There is none here, except on my wife's bookshelves," said Paco. "Any culture they want they must bring with them."

"Do people not play musical instruments here?" Jenny asked.

"Old Ramón still has a trumpet, I think," said María Jesús.

Paco sighed. "Ah, many, many years ago there was a brass band. They played here and in other villages, but even when I was a child it was coming to an end, just a few old men and a couple of boys."

Neil raised his hand. "If the people who come can play music, that will be good."

"But play as a hobby, not as a job," I said, fearing that any hopeful busker would soon become an encumbrance.

Jaime nodded, his face impassive. "Point number six."

Oh, come on, I thought.

"The provision of new housing."

"What? What for?" Paco cried, clearly feeling that Jaime hadn't taken a thing in.

He took off his glasses, wiped them on his sleeve and replaced them with a prod. "If everything goes to plan, two or three years from now we may need to build a few more houses. How do things stand as regards planning permission here, Uncle?"

He made a sweeping gesture. "As far as I'm concerned you can build wherever you like. The last permanent structure built here was Juanjo's new pigsty. Him and his father built that when he got back from doing his military service, thirty-odd years ago."

Jaime nodded. "Well, there will be time enough to decide where the new street will be situated." He looked at his notes. "Those are my major points. I would just like to add that I feel that this initiative is crucial not only to the survival of the village, but to that of Spain as a viable, thriving country. When there is no more petroleum the people will need to know how to live off the land, so our small step here may be a giant one for Spain as a whole."

I noticed he was reading this part.

"After my years of patient study and subsequent disappointments, I feel that I may finally have found my mission in life. Is it destiny?" He shrugged. "I don't know, but I hope that today will be the beginning of something big for our country." He placed his notes in the folder, stood up, made an almost imperceptible little bow, told us he was off for a siesta and almost floated upstairs. We heard the soft thud of a door closing.

As we all looked at each other I was waiting for someone to laugh so that I could join in – quietly, of course – but we remained mute until Paco sighed and said that Jaime had always been an intense little boy and something of a loner.

"While the other children got up to all kinds of mischief, he never wandered far from his house and was often seen muttering to himself. I thought he was simple-minded at first, until he started school and began to do well."

"Did he go to school here?" Jenny asked.

"To primary school, yes," said María Jesús. "It was at the time he began secondary school that they went to live in Madrid."

"What do you think of his ideas?" I asked her, already planning to quash this coup that the pedantic pillock seemed set on making. I hadn't exactly taken a dislike to him as a person, but I didn't wish to see my life shaken up by such an insufferable twerp. So far I'd been exceptionally lucky with my lodgers and I was aware that some day one might arrive who I liked less, but not only was Jaime a person I had little desire to become chummy with, but his apparent efficiency threatened to bring more oddballs to my house and ruin our harmonious lives.

She smiled and shook her head. "Oh, I don't know, Jack. We no longer know him so well, as his visits have been infrequent of late, but I suspect that he has become enthused by this topic and is treating it as if it were a university project or something. No doubt he'll calm down when he sees that it won't be so easy to bring suitable people here."

"And he finds that he has nothing to do here, when what he needs is to get a job and earn some money like a man," Paco added.

"Oh, I think his enthusiasm is great," said Neil, his blue eyes sparkling dangerously. "And it is important that a Spanish person is doing this too, not only us foreigners."

"María Jesús and Paco are Spanish," I pointed out.

"Yes, er... I think I mean a young Spanish person from the city. A person from a place where young people who will come are from. Do you understand?"

We said we did.

The chump beamed. "Yes, if the website is good, then people come." He looked at my perturbed face. "They can come to my house, Jack."

I remembered a statistic I'd recently read. "Neil, there are over a billion websites in the world now. Most of them are seen by very few people." I crossed my fingers under the table. "Jenny, what do you think?"

She giggled. "Paco, tell us what you think first."

"The lad is a *fantasma*," he said, which means ghost, or in this case show-off or fantasist. I explained this to Neil before scratching my nose with finger and thumb to hide my grin.

"No, no," he wailed, shaking his head.

"Yes, yes," Paco boomed, nodding his.

"Keep your voice down, dear," said his wife.

"Pah! Jaime talks but never listens." He wagged his finger at me. "Be careful, Jack. If you give him your hand he'll take it up to the elbow. In his studies he has proven himself to be a clever and competent person, so in this kind of thing he might be effective too. Before you know it your house will be full of all sorts of useless people, hanging around instead of finding a job as God commands."

"Yes, that had occurred to me, Paco. Jenny, what do you think?"

She smiled. "Jaime is all right and his ideas are good, but... but I can't express my thoughts in Spanish right now. I'll tell you later at home."

"OK, but can you give us an idea?" I said.

"I think he can be effective. I think people will come, but I don't know what kind of people. Neil, don't make a lot of promises to Jaime yet."

"Oh, I..."

Her big blue-grey eyes bored into his even bigger and bluer ones. "Mark my words," she said in English.

"Yes, Jenny."

I rubbed my hands together, firmly but discretely, as they were all basically on my side apart from Neil, so he could be the guinea pig if he liked. My cheerful state diminished somewhat when I remembered that Jaime was going to be around all weekend, so I was by no means out of the woods yet.

"María Jesús, thank you for a lovely meal," I said.

"You're welcome, Jack."

Jenny and Neil also expressed their gratitude.

"Do you know what Jaime plans to do this weekend?" I asked Paco.

"In the car he was full of this scheme of his."

"Right, well, he can call on us later, or on Saturday or Sunday afternoon. Jenny and I always work in the mornings."

"I'll bring him round when he wants to come," María Jesús said.

As we said our goodbyes I noticed that Paco gripped Neil by both elbows and whispered something rather intensely.

"What did Paco say just then?" I asked him in the street.

"He said, 'Neil, your house is your home, don't forget that,' I think."

"Can you express your thoughts about Jaime now?" I asked Jenny in my sitting room when Neil had gone upstairs for a rest.

"Yes. I might have been able to say it in Spanish, but it's really something that only affects you and me."

"Go on," I said, rather keen on this link between us.

"What are we, Jack?"

"Who?"

"You and me."

"Er… writers?"

"Exactly. And what do writers do?"

"Er, write? Yes, I'm also concerned that we'll be disturbed at our work."

She laughed. "Hang on. What do we write about?"

"Well, I write about crime." She shook her head. I wondered where she'd get her hair cut when she needed to, or if she'd let it grow. I imagined her with longer hair. "Don't I write about crime?"

"Yes and no. Crimes occur in your books, but there's so much more to your writing than that."

I smiled. "I hope so."

"So what do us writers need, Jack?"

"Peace and quiet. Lots of peace and quiet."

She sighed. "Oh, I'll just tell you. We need inspiration; inspiration and material."

"Ah, I see now. So you think we should observe Jaime closely and then write about him."

She shook her head. "That's what non-writers think writers do. They think we study people and then put them in our books just as they are, as if we had no imagination at all."

I grinned. "I might put Jaime in a book, then kill him off. There'll be so many suspects that the reader won't have a clue who did it."

"Ha ha, very good. Anyway, I think Jaime and anyone else he brings to the village will be a good source of inspiration. As writers we should welcome anything new and unusual in our lives, but there's something else too. This project that you, Paco and María Jesús came up with is a wonderful idea."

"Which I don't want Jaime to hijack."

"No, we don't want that, but as writers we do need something else to occupy ourselves, or at least I do. When I finish my work for the day I need to switch off and think about something completely different."

"Yes, well, that's why I go for walks and do little jobs and… things."

"And does that help you to switch off?"

Yes, because I think about you, I thought. "Sometimes," I said.

"Well I go for a walk and I still think about my writing." She shook her head. "One reason I came here was to get away from a social life that always involved literary chitchat. I've done that, but I need something else to keep me busy. I'm all for this project and if Jaime helps to bring a few more people then it'll really have taken off. Now it's just three foreigners, and there's no lack of those in Spain." She shrugged. "We should at least give him a chance, don't you think?"

"Oh, yes, I'm all for giving him a chance too," I said, although if Jenny had been as sceptical as I was about him, I might have stalled until Neil could lodge him. "I wonder when he'll come round."

"Later on, I expect. He's ever so keen and he's bound to want to discuss things with us."

22

Jenny proved to be wrong on both counts. He didn't appear until noon the following day, and he came to proclaim rather than discuss.

"Hola, Jaime," I said dully as I opened the door. "Neil is out drawing and Jenny and I are both working, as I told you we would be."

He tapped his watch and smiled. "I believe that the afternoon begins at midday in England."

"I'm Scottish and we're in Spain, but come in anyway."

He wiped his feet carefully on the mat and I led him towards my sitting room.

"Jenny is still working," I murmured. "She normally writes until two, as do I."

I indicated the sofa but he made for the dining table, where he sat down and opened his folder. Then the door that I'd just closed opened.

"Hola, Jaime, I thought it was you," said Jenny cheerfully.

"Don't interrupt your work," I muttered in English. I would rather have entertained Jaime alone in order to respond in a lukewarm manner to whatever he had in the folder, but Jenny said she'd worked enough and was eager to think about something else, as per her affirmation of the previous day.

The front door opened and closed and I cursed my luck. Neil soon appeared, doffed his sweaty cap, and scampered off to freshen up. So it was that at 1218 hours we were all assembled to hear what our self-appointed leader had to say. At 1251 hours his droning ceased and he finally opened the folder. He'd basically said the same as the previous day, with a few embellishments and no questions. Neil smiled and nodded throughout this monologue, while Jenny took a few notes, not about his mind-numbing spiel, she confessed later, but about his voice, expressions and mannerisms.

"So, as I said, I've been working on our website." He extracted some sheets. "As I didn't bring my laptop I've made some notes by hand, so please tell me what you think of them. May I use the bathroom, Jack?"

I told him where it was and he went.

"He likes to make these timely exits," I said. "Now, let's see… bloody hell, look at this."

I gazed at my friends while they gaped at Jaime's handiwork. Have you ever seen photos of those little books that the Brontë siblings made when they were kids, in tiny, precise handwriting with little maps and other illustrations? Well, each of Jaime's sheets looked a bit like them, divided into columns and with sketches where he intended to put photos.

"I think each sheet is supposed to represent a webpage," Jenny murmured as she strained her lovely eyes.

"Yes, one of those with too much on them," said the cynic.

"I'll need to get my reading specs, but it looks brilliant," said the optimist.

"I see he's left no room whatsoever to make changes."

"He must have stayed up half the night to do this," said Jenny.

"It's just a rough draft," said Jaime, who had glided silently in. I hadn't asked him if he spoke English, but I suspected he didn't, or not very well. This suited me fine, as if nothing else he gave us a chance to practise our Spanish.

"It's fantastic," said his biggest fan. "You have done a lot of work."

He shrugged. "I'm used to it. So, if you approve of the content I'll create the website when I get home, then post links to it from several social media sites." He smiled. "I'm confident that within a few days some suitable people will have contacted me."

"I want to speak to anyone who might wish to stay in this house, preferably by video call," I said.

"Of course. Once I've made an initial selection, I'll tell them to contact you."

"Er, but what if someone you reject is someone who I might like?"

He gazed at me like a patient priest. "That is unlikely. I have all our interests at heart."

Neil raised his hand. "One month from now I have my house. For me a practical person is good, to help me do some work. For that they will pay no rent and I give them food."

"Very good, Neil. Ideally the people who come will be both dextrous and conscious of the importance of our mission."

"I don't mind if someone comes who doesn't care about the mission, or isn't very clever, as long as they have an occupation," I said.

"Yes, you said." He looked at his watch. "My aunt is expecting me for lunch, so if you can find the time to read the content of the website I'll come later and we can discuss it in more detail." He placed the sheets in the middle of the table and stood up.

"As I had to stop work early this morning I will have to work this afternoon too," I said, just to show him the grumpy sort of guy he might be lodging with. "I imagine Jenny will also have to make up for lost time," I added, shooting her a brotherly glance.

"I… yes, I may do a little more later."

"I will be free," said Neil. "I will read this now."

"Very good. I'll see myself out." He nodded and was gone.

At 1627 hours the bugger was back. I know the exact time because when Neil greeted him effusively I looked at my bedside clock before turning over and trying to get back to sleep, until the following morning if possible. I tossed, turned and grumbled for a while, before getting up, shaving, taking a long shower, dressing slowly, looking out of the window, combing my still short hair in three different ways and finally descending the stairs. He'd been there for an hour and was still on the first page of his proto-website, droning away. Neil's eyes looked a bit glazed but he was smiling and nodding. Jenny held a small pad in her hand, but her fatigued expression bucked me up somewhat. She was cracking.

I daren't go into much detail about the next two hours, because I want those of you who've read this far to finish the book. To sum up, he droned and droned, paid lip service to our comments and said nothing new. It was clear to me that he was in love with the sound of his own voice. When he finally shoved those damn sheets into the folder I suggested that we'd discussed things enough for the time being.

"Oh, but I may make some revisions this evening. Your input has been most helpful."

Even Neil looked doubtful.

"Well, tomorrow I'll be working *all* morning, but feel free to call round in the afternoon, after six. We could go for a walk or go to the bar and have a nice chat about all sorts of things."

"Yes, we still don't know very much about you, Jaime," said my ally.

"Yes, we can have a drink in the bar for you to speak to the village men," said his.

"We will see." He stood up. "Hasta mañana." He left.

"Neil?" I said when the front door had closed.
"Yes?"
"You *must* be getting bored of him by now."

His lips curled up, but not much. "This afternoon he's been a bit repetitive, but he wants to get the website right."

"Can you imagine living with him?" I asked them both.

Jenny shrugged and slapped her pad shut. "I doubt I'll get much more out of him now. To be honest I'd rather someone else came to stay, but we can't very well turn him away, can we?"

"He can stay at mine, a month from now," said Neil.

"He can stay here until then, I suppose. Hey, what about this interview he's got?" I smiled for the first time in a while. "He might get the job, then our troub… dilemma will be over."

"He'll probably flunk it on purpose now that he's found his calling," said J.

"He won't do that. He's not that kind of person," said N.

"I doubt he'll get it anyway," I said. "He'll bore them to tears. He hasn't said when he's coming to stay yet. It might not be for a while."

Neil tutted. "He told me. Next weekend, he said."

I sighed.

"He might be different tomorrow, more relaxed. We'll have to try to steer the conversation onto other things," said Jenny.

When the knock on the door came at half past five the following afternoon I jumped up from the sofa and hurried into the patio, where I prised the lid from a tin of light green paint and began to add to the small section of the end wall that I'd painted that morning, just as a warm-up. I was not prepared to sit at that table with him for a single moment, thus my cunning contingency plan. When Jenny scuttled out I handed her a brush and we began to labour side by side. Neil called from inside, but we went on painting.

"Ah, there you are," he said as he led out our leader.

"Grab a brush if you like. We're just going to finish this wall."

"I was going to do that with a roller," Neil said in English.

"With four of us it will not take so long," Jaime said in English.

"I didn't know you spoke English," I said in Spanish, because him droning on in our mother tongue really would be the straw that broke the Scotsman's back.

He shrugged. "I speak English quite well, but you all need to practise Castilian, so I will not speak it."

Relieved, I handed him a brush and for the next half hour he painted with arm outstretched to preserve his shiny shoes. He did his bit though, so by the time we'd washed our hands and headed off to the bar he'd gone up in my estimations.

Paco's place was quite full, so I suggested we sit outside in the shade. By the time I'd brought a jug of beer and a few nibbles, Jaime had opened the dreaded folder and I considered returning to the bar for a bottle of Scotch. As I said, I'm no great drinker, but it occurred to me that if I polished off half a bottle of Johnny Walker, sang *The Bonnie Banks o' Loch Lomond* at the top of my voice and then slumped to the ground, he might be less keen to stay with me.

I needn't have worried, because after drinking half an inch of beer he announced that he was going inside to talk to the men about our project. He took his folder with him, so I rubbed my hands together and tuned in to gauge the audible reaction to his incursion. The volume fell, a droning voice was heard, then business as usual was resumed. I expected him to return to us with head bowed, ignored by the masses, but Jenny, who faced the window, then regaled us with a running commentary.

"Ah, I see. I think his plan is to take each of them aside and explain it to them. I don't know the old man he's talking to now, but he's staring at Jaime as if he were a madman… he's gone back to the bar. Now he's backing Toni towards the wall… he seems to be listening… oh, he pointed at the telly and left him. I think the football is about to begin. Ooh, it's Juanjo's turn now. At least he isn't so keen on football. Isn't he sweet when you try to explain something to him? He's listening patiently… uh-oh, his mouth's starting to droop… he's… gone to the toilet. Now Jaime's collared that nice gay man."

"Enrique."

"Yes, Enrique. He nods... he smiles... he nods... he smiles… he looks out of the window. Oh, he's looking at me and pulling a funny face. Smiling again… but he's obviously bored to death."

"He'll be the death of our bloody project, that… one," I snapped. "What's *he* going to achieve after Paco's spoken to every man jack of them already? Even we can promote the project better than him. To them he probably seems more foreign than we are. Oh dear, it's not looking good, is it?"

"I thought he had a way with people, but he seems to be having little luck with the blokes," Neil said sadly. "I never expected this response."

"You know, I think he reminds them too much of politicians," said Jenny. "I was watching some on telly the other day and he seems a lot like them from where I'm sitting."

"Yes, and most of the blokes hate them, as they do sod all for the rural areas," I said.

About then we began to receive feedback regarding his endeavours, as I think some of the men were off to watch the football at home. Happily none of the half dozen who left connected the dismal orator with us, so we heard a few muttered curses and one snippet of conversation between two of the summer men.

"Who the devil is that little *gilipollas*?"

"It's Serrano's lad."

"What's he been doing?"

"Studying, for years."

"It's f*cked his head up."

"Yes, it seems so. What was he on about?"

"Dunno, something about fetching some of his pals here to stay."

"Oh, God help us. I come here to relax, not listen to waffle."

Jaime, however, appeared to be oblivious to his poor reception and didn't emerge until our jug was empty and every single man immersed in the football, forming a tight Jaime-proof pack around the bar.

"Good talks?" Neil asked him.

"Not bad. Like most village men they resist change, but I could see a spark of interest in their eyes." He smiled. "Yes, once I'm living here I'll be able to come often and eventually convince them that each household must host a lodger, if not two."

Neil nodded, Jenny smiled in a rather petrified way and I went to the loo, or tried to, because Paco came around the bar, grasped my arm and led me into the kitchen.

"The bar is busy this evening," I said.

He glowered. "Yes, but only because those who don't have satellite TV have had to stay to watch the match. Oh, that Jaime is worse than I thought, much worse. If he comes here regularly he'll drive the men away. I sit here through the winter, dreaming of the summer. When I clear the snow from the doorway and only Juanjo and Toni come, I tell myself, you're doing the right thing, Paco, keeping the bar open and the village alive."

I tutted empathically. "He probably won't come here very often."

"No?"

"No."

"Not ten minutes ago he told me he intended to come here *every* evening, Jack." His brown eyes bulged. "He'll find lodgings for all his people if it kills him, he said, but it'll kill me, not him."

I patted his arm. "Calm down, Paco."

"Ach, if he weren't family, of sorts, I'd drive him to Cuenca station right now."

"But he is doing what we all want to do, isn't he?"

"In the wrong way, Jack. I told you that little by little is the way to go, didn't I?"

"Yes, and I agree." I smiled. "Anyway, he might be successful at his interview on Tuesday."

"Would you employ that... sanctimonious babbler?"

"It would depend, but I'd probably want to keep him away from people."

"Please keep him away from my people then, Jack." One of the blokes called him. "Wait!"

"What, er... will his family think about this project, do you think?"

"His parents want him to find a job. He's never had a job, not even a little one in summer. They'll see this as an attempt to avoid getting one. He's been a drain on their resources for a long time now and if he comes here they'll have to go on giving him money."

I thought about the €600 I'd received from Neil and Jenny (400 + 200) and feared that Jaime might gobble those funds up, literally.

Paco sighed. "His friends have followed the well-trodden path of many Spaniards in times of hardship and gone abroad to make some money, but not him."

I then had a minor brainwave. Nothing fancy, just the work of a few stray neurons, but a couple of things that had been on my mind suddenly came together in a most interesting way.

"So you say Jaime's parents are desperate for him to get a job?"

"Hmm, desperate, I don't know, but extremely eager."

I squeezed his arm. "I may have a plan. See you later."

On stepping outside I saw that Jenny seemed extremely eager to go home, as Jaime had opened the Folder from Hell and was droning once more. Neil's smile was like that of a vicar listening to a parishioner's trifling troubles for the twentieth time. I yawned loudly as I sat down.

"I must be off to bed soon."

"Me too," said Jenny.

"It's only half past nine," *he* said.

"Jenny and I always begin work at six. Our work means a lot to us, and we need to earn money, like everybody else."

Neil stood up and stretched. Good man, I thought.

"Well, Jaime, best of luck at the interview," I said as I offered my hand.

He touched it and shrugged. "I'll try my best, as always, but I'll be myself, as always. It will be my fourteenth interview. I fully expect to see you next weekend."

Neil shook his hand. "See you then."

Jenny kissed his cheeks. "See you soon."

"See you later," I said, and we left without paying, but I'd reckon up with Paco the following evening, when I hoped to have some promising news.

"There's a strange glint in your eyes, Jack," Jenny said as we strolled up the street.

"What time is it in Britain now?"

"Just after half past eight."

"Then I must walk up towards the woods," I murmured, waving my usually useless mobile phone.

"Who are you going to call?"

"Nicola, my ex. I feel that she owes me one," I said, but before taking my twilight stroll I realised that I ought to apprise them of my intentions.

"Oh, I don't know about that," was Neil's response to my dastardly ploy.

"Do it," was Jenny's. "Sometimes one has to be cruel to be kind, and what you propose may well be for the best."

I gazed at Neil. He raised his hands and let them fall. "All right, if you think she can pull it off."

"She has contacts. See you shortly."

23

On my way up towards the woods I wondered if I should have consulted María Jesús, but there was no time to lose. I was sure that Paco would soon be sharing his woes with her and that his mental and physical well-being took precedence over anything else, so as soon as I got a half-decent signal I called Nicola's mobile for the first time since arriving in Spain.

"Hello, Nicola, it's me."

"Well, hello, Jack," she said, surprised.

"I'm not disturbing you, am I?"

"No, as a matter of fact I'm at the house, picking up a few things."

"Ah, good. Are you well?"

"Yes, I'm fine. And you? You didn't answer my email."

"I will, soon."

"Yes, I would like us to stay in touch, Jack."

"Yes, and we will. Did you get the money I sent?"

"Yes, thanks, but don't send any more. I might be sending you some, in fact, as I'm going to rent this place out and it turns out that I'll get well over a thousand a month."

My mouth watered. "Oh no, Nicola, a deal's a deal. Ha, I've got a couple of lodgers at my place, as a matter of fact," I said, before briefly outlining our project.

"Oh, that's really good. Who's staying with you?"

"An artist from Yorkshire called Neil and a promising young writer from Derbyshire called Jenny. We get on fine and don't disturb each other at work, so it's working out well."

"Great. How's the book going?"

"Oh, really well. I've had some excellent feedback, so it should sell well. Is everything OK with you?"

"Yes, I'm fine," she said, knowing that I hated the sound of her doctor's name, but I now had Jenny, under my roof at least.

"Is... Stuart well?"

"Yes, he's fine. Thanks for asking." She chuckled. "Did you call for any particular reason, Jack?"

"Well, yes. I want to ask a rather peculiar favour of you."

"Go on."

After quickly spelling out the situation, I told her what I wanted her to do.

"Hmm, right, but so quickly?"

"If possible, yes. I'll be really grateful if you can manage it."

"I'll speak to dad now, if you're absolutely sure."

"Yes, I'm sure. It's the best solution for all concerned."

"All right, I'll call him. I know they're busy at the moment."

I asked her to drop me an email and after we'd uttered a few more pleasantries I hung up and clenched my free fist.

Good old Nicola, a traitorous wife but still a friend. She wasn't as pretty as Jenny and living with such a keen lawyer had been a bore at times, but she was reliable and although she'd broken her marriage vows I knew she'd keep this promise. I jest, but it had been nice to speak to her now that my life was going well. Maybe Jenny and I would go to their wedding and they would come to ours, I mused half-seriously as I loped back to the house. Neil had prepared a cold supper and they awaited me in my sitting room.

"Sorted," I said.

"Already?" said Neil.

"As good as. I always got on well with Nicola's dad, so I'm sure he'll be happy to help."

"But that's only half the battle, Jack," said Jenny.

"Hmm, true. When I get the nod from Nicola I'll speak to María Jesús. We can count on her to set the wheels in motion." I sat down at the table. "Ah, it's not what you know but who you know."

Neil frowned. "I still think it's a bit cruel."

"You know the saying, Neil," said Jenny.

"Yes, I do."

We tucked in.

Nicola emailed me on Tuesday afternoon – at about the time of Jaime's interview, funnily enough – and said that her father could offer three options, provided I was sure that this brainy Spaniard would be sure to stick at it. I grabbed my phone and headed not for the best mobile signal spot, but to the bar. I greeted Juanjo, who I noticed had finally addressed his nose and ear hair issue, and asked Paco if María Jesús was in.

"Yes."

"I may have some good news for you soon," I said, before stepping outside and knocking on the house door.

Over coffee I spelt out the options.

"I see. Are you absolutely sure that he'll be all right there?" she said.

"Yes, Nicola's father will arrange the job and she has promised to sort out his accommodation and keep an eye on him."

"Right. So, he can work in a hotel, a cafe or an office?"

"Yes, Nicola will take him to see her father and they will have a sort of informal interview. He has friends in the hotel business, but I think the office job at his company is the best. They have customers in South America, so his Spanish will be useful there, and I really can't see him in the other two roles."

"No, too many people to deal with." She smiled and nodded slowly. "It all seems too easy."

"Not really. There are lots of jobs in Glasgow just now, for those who want to do them. He will soon meet other Spaniards there, and as I say, Nicola will make sure he's all right." I sipped my coffee. "Now the rest is up to you."

She nodded pensively. "Hmm, I think I can arrange it, but it's a little tricky. I wonder whether I should speak to his mother first or to him. If I speak to her it may seem like a trap, but if I speak to him he'll know that I'll tell her if he makes excuses." She gazed at me. "You may not come out of this very well in Jaime's eyes, Jack."

I shrugged. "I'm prepared to take that risk. We don't want him here. He will ruin our project and after a few weeks he will be fed up anyway. He needs to get a job, make some money and… make wider his horizons."

"That's true. I'll call him later to ask about the interview. Once he's told me how stupid they were not to employ him, I'll present him with this Scottish option."

"How will you go about it?"

She pursed her lips and drummed her neatly manicured nails on the table. "Well, I'll say that you happened to speak to your wife about him, telling her how intelligent and able he is, and she… are you sure about this office job?"

"Nicola seemed to be. Her father needs people."

"Right, well let's forget about the other two jobs for now." She chuckled. "That would seem like a conspiracy. So, you told your wife about him and she immediately mentioned this job. It sounded ideal for him and you told me. I'll tell him I was about to call his mother, but decided to call him first. That will make him think. Yes, I believe it will work."

"Tell him that Nicola will meet him at the airport and look after him. He might stay in my old house at first."

"That's very kind of her."

I shrugged. "She feels… in debt to me."

She looked at the clock on the wall. "Shall I call him now?"

"Er, if you want."

She laughed. "I won't tell him you're here." She fetched the house phone, found his number and dialled.

She was masterful. She allowed him to speak very little and the way she combined enthusiasm, persuasive powers and the subtly veiled threat of calling his mother was a joy to hear. Towards the end of the ten-minute call she sounded like a motivational speaker and after finally hearing him out for a minute or two she said goodbye and hung up.

"How did he take it?" I asked.

"Better than I expected. He didn't get that job, of course, so I think I caught him at a vulnerable moment. Every time he goes home after an interview there are long faces, I believe. You know, he didn't mention the project once. He says he may go, but he wants to speak to Nicola first."

I gulped. "Right, yes, I understand that. I'll go and call her now."

"Use our phone."

"Thanks." I dialled. Nicola was in her office at the law firm and sounded pleased that Jaime had responded positively.

"My dad really does need someone bright right now, he says."

I asked her to call Jaime and warned her that he was apt to be a tad pedantic, but I assured her that his great logical and analytical powers would be a sterling asset to any company.

"If your dad sits him down at a computer and gives him something really challenging to do, he'll be amazed by what he's capable of. He has a huge capacity for work... yes, his English is pretty good and I think he speaks some French too. I'm really grateful for this, Nicola."

"You're welcome. I'll call him and set the ball rolling."

"Thanks a lot. I'll be in touch." I hung up.

"Well?"

"So far so good. Nicola can be quite charming, so with any luck he will be flying off to Scotland soon."

She sighed.

"It's a beautiful country, you know, and I'm sure Malcolm, Nicola's father, will pay him well."

"Perhaps at last Jaime will become a man."

"And we will go on as before."

She chuckled. "I suppose he'll have put you off getting more lodgers."

I shrugged. "This month I must work a lot."

"And next month Neil will have his house."

I smiled. "That's right."

I feel – and you may well agree – that Jaime has occupied us for long enough now, so rather than posting intermittent updates regarding his progress, I'll jump ahead a little in order to conclude his participation in this account. About a week after María Jesús's fateful call he jetted off to Glasgow and began work at my ex-father-in-law's company, where he soon got up to speed and was well-liked despite, or maybe because of, his quirky ways. After staying in my former home for a couple of weeks, he moved into a nice house with three more Spaniards and the last I heard was that he'd been knocking about at the university with a view to beginning his doctoral studies on a part-time basis. All's well that ends well, and we all felt good about the way things had turned out, especially me. He never called to thank me for giving him his start in life, but I didn't mind too much.

Thanks to him Nicola and I were speaking again, and I promised to arrange the transportation of my books before long, lest her new tenants take a fancy to any of them.

24

So life got back to normal and the three of us worked around the hot August weather. We usually got up at the crack of dawn and after a quick breakfast Jenny and I would accompany Neil to his drawing spot in the hills, in order to stretch our legs before getting down to work. The ground floor remained reasonably cool most days and as Jenny plodded on with her novel I finished my third and began my fourth and final revision. We lunched together, napped apart, and normally took another stroll before having pre-dinner drinks on Paco's makeshift terrace. It was a pleasant, satisfying routine and as Neil had begun to try his hand at watercolours, he too felt creative and industrious, while his occasional bike rides kept him in trim.

One sultry evening Jenny finally presented us both with copies of the story which had won her a prize, and as it was quite short we both agreed to read it later in bed.

She placed her hands on her cheeks. "Oh, I hope you like it. I value your opinion more than the critics' and judges'."

"Why's that, Jenny?" Neil asked.

"Because you're both normal, intelligent readers, the sort of people my novel's aimed at."

"So why not let us read some of that?" I asked with a cheeky grin.

"Oh no, not yet. If you didn't like it I'd be distraught."

"I'm sure it's great," said Neil.

"Who will you show it to?" I asked, picturing John Smith's sneering face.

"No-one at all until I've finished the first draft, then... well, you two, I suppose."

Neil and I were both chuffed about this and I'm sure he hoped as anxiously as I did that Jenny's style hadn't been corrupted by the pretentious literary coterie she'd been rubbing shoulders with for several years.

"Would you like to read my third draft?" I asked them.

"I'd love to," said Jenny. "I'm dying to see how your detective's getting on."

"Yes, and I want to see if you've heeded my humble advice," said Neil.

I laughed. "I think you'll like the way the dagger goes in now."

"No twisting?"

"No twisting, but... well, you'll see."

When I turned out the bedside light that night I felt a great sense of relief. Jenny's prize-winning story was a plotless bit of nonsense, written to impress the judges, as she'd confessed, but she couldn't half write. Her style was essentially simple but elegant, her descriptions short and original, her dialogues natural, and there were just enough sapient sentences to prove that if she chose to avoid obscure words it was because she had little use for them. I considered tiptoeing into her room, slipping into bed beside her and whispering in her ear, 'Jenny, you're brilliant and I want you to stay here forever and ever,' before kissing her tenderly.

In the event, because she must have known that I'd have read her story, I did get up, tied my dressing down tightly around me and went to tap on her door, just to tell her how talented she was. On my way there I bumped into a shadowy man creeping suspiciously in the same direction.

"Are you going to do the same as me?" he whispered.

"Er, I hope so."

I tapped and he softly called her name.

"Come in."

There she was, sitting up in bed in a pretty nightie with a book of poetry open on her lap.

"We... er, you first, Neil."

"I think your story's wonderful, Jenny. You write brilliantly."

She lowered her eyes and blushed.

"After reading it I'm sure your novel's going to be great," I said.

"Oh, thank goodness for that. I don't think I'd have slept tonight." She sniffled a bit. "Oh, thank you so much, it's such a relief."

We wished her goodnight and closed the door.

"Great minds think alike, eh, Jack?"

"Yes, goodnight, Neil."

Neil was no slouch at his recently purchased easel either, as after a fortnight of watercolouring he'd begun to produce some decent little pictures. Jenny told him so the next morning over breakfast.

"Oh, you're just saying that," he said, flapping a hand that seemed too large to effect such fine brushstrokes.

She laughed. "Why, because you flattered me about my story? No, seriously, with a bit more practice I'm sure you could paint pictures that would sell."

"Aw, give over. It's just a hobby to keep me out of mischief. I just paint the same old scenes over and over again."

"That's as it should be," I said sagely. "It's good to keep at it till you get them right, but feel free to take the car and paint wherever you like. You know, I doubt there are many artists painting around here, so you might find a market for your work."

"Restaurants, bars," said Jenny.

"Rural lodgings, village halls, private buyers," I added.

"Not big pictures and not too expensive."

"Frame them yourself. You're handy enough to make a good job of it."

"Market days in Molina and Beteta," she said, as we'd been to both by then.

Neil smiled at this stereophonic assault and admitted that he wouldn't mind augmenting his pension a bit. "But not yet. I'll practise all winter and maybe in the spring I'll have something worth selling. I'd rather do things right, like you two do."

"It'll seem strange here when you go to live in your house," Jenny said, causing my neck to tingle strangely.

"Oh, I imagine you'll see almost as much of me as you do now, me being so close."

"You must come to eat with us often," she said.

"And you with me."

I smiled. "Will you want to find a lodger to keep you company?"

He sipped his milky coffee and smacked his lips. "Hmm, I'm still up for it, but like Paco says, little by little. There's no hurry and we've spread the word to the summer folk, so when they go home they might come across people who'd like to give it a go. I think they should take the initiative anyway, rather than us persuading them to come."

"I agree," I said. "What do you think, Jenny?"

She smiled diffidently. "It's not for me to say really. I'm still not sure what I'm going to do after October. I'll go to the festival, as I promised, but..." She shrugged and munched her last bit of toast.

I looked at my watch. "Shall we set off?" I said, as it was too early in the morning to put her on the spot.

They chattered away as we walked up the hill, Neil toting his easel and Jenny his painting satchel, while I walked behind them, mulling over her inconclusive words. I had no idea if she'd been in touch with John Smith. She rarely wandered off alone in the evenings, so they might not have been speaking much, if at all, but I imagined she'd at least been in contact by email, although I'd noticed no mood swings whatsoever. Since she'd said that she didn't want to talk about him, neither Neil nor I had uttered his name in her presence, or together for that matter, but as the end of August approached I began to dwell on her possible departure more and more. I could handle Neil leaving the house, as he'd only be three doors away, but if Jenny packed up and moved on I knew she'd leave a gap that would be hard to fill, irrespective of whether or not we ever became more than friends. My conduct towards her had always been chivalrous and at times even a little aloof, but she was surely aware of my feelings for her, or was she?

The crucial factor, of course, was where she stood with John Smith, so it might be best to try to ascertain that before making a fool of myself by imploring her to stay. I would have a word with Neil first, I decided, but there was no hurry as it was still over a month to D-day, or J-day. The literary festival began in about the middle of October, but she'd probably go home to Derbyshire first, and then perhaps to London...

"Have you had a great idea for your book, Jack?" Neil said over his shoulder. "You look lost in thought."

I laughed weakly. "No, I can't change anything much now. I... I was thinking about what I'm going to write next."

We soon reached Neil's latest painting spot, overlooking the village and fields with a long, wooded sierra in the distance. After Jenny had fussed around a bit, making sure he had sun cream, enough water and something to eat, we set off back down the hill.

"He'll be able to paint some snowy scenes in winter, I expect," I said.

"Yes, I think it'll be more interesting for an artist then, with longer shadows or cloudy skies. He is quite good, isn't he?"

"I'm no expert, but he's certainly becoming competent and can only get better. I'll order some firewood for the stove soon," I said, my speech evidently taking its instructions directly from my subconscious mind.

"Already? But it's still boiling hot."

"Yes, but Paco says it's better to buy soon, to make sure of getting dry wood. If they run out the next lot might be green, you see, and that doesn't burn so well."

"Ah, I see. It's hard to imagine it being cold and snowy right now, isn't it?"

"Yes, but it will be, especially after Christmas, I believe. Good writing weather, though. How much of your novel have you done?"

She giggled. "That depends on how long it's going to be, as I'm no longer sticking strictly to my scheme, but I think I've written about 150 book pages, so I guess there's about half of it left to write. A good winter's work anyway, and then the rewriting. How about you?"

"After this last revision I'll send it to Samantha, my agent. If she's satisfied she'll send it to my publisher and that'll be that. Then I'll be able to start something new."

"Another crime novel?"

"No, not yet. The truth is that I've discovered I can knock those off quite quickly, so I'll write something a bit… deeper first, I think; something to really get stuck into over the winter."

She laughed. "Then if I'm still here we'll both be hard at it."

I couldn't help but smile radiantly.

She frowned. "But I'm not sure about that yet, Jack. It'll depend on… a number of things."

"Ha, yes, of course, no sweat."

"Whatever I decide to do, I'll leave a few things here anyway, if that's all right with you, as I'm bound to come to visit."

I pictured myself lying naked on my bed with her clothes strewn over me, sobbing disconsolately. "Yes, of course, you'll always be welcome."

"Here we are." She pushed open the door and sighed. "Time to get down to it, I suppose."

"Yes. Coffee at ten?"

"That would be lovely."

Revising a novel for the fourth time is easy work if you're satisfied with it. It's more a question of proofreading than anything else, and as I slowly mouthed each word I was thankful that I wasn't engaged in real creative work, as I'd have found it awfully hard to concentrate after my chat with Jenny. Her response to my radiant smile suggested that she was aware that I longed for her to stay. She may, therefore, guess the nature of my feelings for her, but did she have any such feelings for me? Would I wait until she was about to board the plane before telling her what she meant to me, or would I be a man and spell it out to her sooner?

Sooner, much sooner, I decided, before reading one of the few love scenes in my story for the last time.

25

A few days later I had a conversation which snapped me out of the rather maudlin mood I'd been in as I trudged towards the bar for a post-siesta coffee. Jenny and Neil were completing the painting of the patio walls, joshing each other regarding their broad-brush styles, so I left them to it and went for a quick pick-me-up. On the way there I saw Juan Carlos, Pablo the builder's son and heir, chipping the crumbling cement off a house wall. He hailed me cheerfully, so I walked over.

"Hola, Juan Carlos, how's it going?"

"Not bad, Jack. Just preparing this wall for rendering. They've finally decided to smarten the old place up," said the tanned, strapping chap in his early thirties. He told me the house belonged to a summer family who lived near the Catalan coast. I asked after his father.

"He's pricing a job at a house over past the church."

"Summer people?"

"Ha, yes. They're the ones with the money."

"So has it been a bit busier than usual this summer?"

"July was steady, but this month has been hectic." He smiled and shook his glistening head. "No holiday for us for a while, though we'll try to get away for a week before the kids go back to school."

"Why is there so much work now?"

"Well, I think there's a bit of rivalry, you know. One finally decides to get some work done, so another feels he has to as well. Ha, it suits us fine."

"Why this summer, do you think?"

"Well, maybe you and Neil coming has made folk think that the village must be a pretty good place after all."

I smiled, having received the answer I'd been angling for. I decided to cast for another. I doubt I'd spoken to Juan Carlos more than half a dozen times and never for long, so at the risk of appearing to be a busybody I asked him if he still planned to move to Cuenca before his elder daughter started secondary school.

He rubbed his head with the back of his hand and grimaced. "Well, that's still the plan, but my wife's beginning to have second thoughts, and she's the one who has to drive them to school."

I nodded encouragingly. Go on, go on, I thought, tell me that it's because of me, me, me.

"If we keep getting as much work as we have been doing it'll be a wrench to move there and start from scratch. Our parents are all for us staying, of course, so we'll just have to see."

"We hope to encourage more Spanish people to come here. It was Paco's idea, but we're helping him."

"Good, good." He sniffed and wrinkled his nose. "Wasn't Serrano's son here, talking about that? I heard he'd been pestering folk in the bar."

I shook my head. "No... well, yes, he was here, but he's just gone to Scotland to work. I... helped to arrange it."

He smiled. "Ah."

"Yes, all *we* are doing is trying to encourage people to move here who might be able to make a living." I shrugged and scrunched up my face in the Spanish way. "Maybe no-one else will come this year. Little by little, you know."

"And what about that lovely young woman who's staying with you? Is she just here for the summer or for longer?"

I blushed in the Scottish way. "Oh, she might stay. She's not sure yet."

He smiled. "Are you and her... you know?" he said, pressing two fingers together.

"Oh, we're just friends."

Seeing my discomfiture, he turned to examine his handiwork. "Yes, you coming has been a good thing for the village. I'd better get on with this now."

"OK, Juan Carlos, see you later."

By the time I reached the bar my skin had cooled and the fact that Juan Carlos and his family might end up staying was uppermost in my mind. I told Paco and Juanjo about it.

"Yes, his father told me he was having a change of heart," Paco said as he prepared my coffee.

"It's because of all the work they've got," said Juanjo, resplendent in a rose-coloured shirt.

As we were alone, I decided to tease him a little.

"You're looking smart, Juanjo. Do you have plans for the evening?"

He cleared his throat, but didn't blush. "Yes, I'm taking my friend Veronica to Beteta for dinner."

"This place is no longer good enough for you, eh?" said the boss.

"For me, yes, but you know what women are like." He shrugged. "There's a nice place she likes there, so we'll go."

I glanced at the door. "Is it true that you may be going to live with her in Valencia?"

He bridled. "To Valencia, me? Ha, not likely." He prodded the bar. "I live here."

Paco smiled. "That's true."

"I mean in the village." He smoothed his shirt. "It is possible that I may go to visit her there occasionally, but to live, never. Cuenca is far too busy for me, so Valencia must be hell."

"She might come to live here," I said, as he'd intimated as much to Neil.

"She might, in a year or two, God willing."

I patted his arm. "I'm glad."

He smoothed his sleeve and grunted. "And you and Jenny, what?"

"Just friends." I drank up, slapped a coin on the bar and told them I had to get back to my work.

On my return I saw through the rear window that they'd just finished the wall and were sitting in the shade, chatting, laughing and gesticulating with their paint-smeared hands. It was all right for Neil, I thought, because due to his age he could chill out and be himself, the lucky old sod.

It was when they told me they'd both just finished reading my third draft that I began to find their palliness a bit irksome. During the last week or so I'd noticed how often I came across them together, always relaxed and chatty, like friends who'd known each other for years rather than a few weeks. Not only had they finished reading the story at the same time, but they appeared to have discussed it already.

"You've made those changes we talked about very well and I think it's a splendid book," he said.

"I think it's even better than the last one, so you've a good chance of creating a really successful series," she said.

"Thanks. Is there anything you didn't like? I'm on the last revision now, but it isn't too late to change things."

After conferring with a glance they each mentioned the same secondary character.

"I don't think he should wear a tie at that dinner," said Neil.

"No, it seems a bit out of character, and when he's walking out in a huff I think he might stare rather than glare at the woman."

"And then just snort rather than utter a curse."

I laughed. "All right. Is that all?"

"Yes," they said in unison.

"I'll be coming to that bit soon, so I'll make those changes. Thanks for being so thorough," I said, grateful and annoyed in equal measure. Neil seemed much closer to Jenny than I was and I couldn't help but resent it. Perhaps he had a better idea of what she planned to do in October though, so I'd ask him the next time I got him alone.

26

What with one thing and another I didn't have that chat until we were in the middle of his house move at the beginning of September, which was mostly a question of carrying his things round and rearranging the furniture to his liking.

"Do you want us to empty the rooms you're going to do some work on?" I asked him in the big old kitchen one morning, as he'd spoken of retiling floors, varnishing doors, painting walls and suchlike.

"Oh, I don't think so, Jack. Now I'm here I can see there's nothing really urgent to do and I'll have all winter to do it. Ha, I think all those years of enforced DIY have put me off it a bit. Here I can do what the hell I want. That crack in the ceiling, for instance. I can sit here drinking coffee and think, I'll fix that crack when I flaming well feel like it, not when someone nags me about it."

"That's true. You know, it'll seem strange you being here and me and Jenny being there. I think you're closer to her than I am," I said, wondering if she might really prefer to spend her final weeks with him.

He scratched his head and looked into my eyes. "Do you think so, Jack?"

"Well, you seem to spend more time with her than I do."

"Yes, er... is she working now?"

"Yes, she wanted to do a couple of hours before lunch."

"Let's sit down for a mo. Sorry I can't offer you coffee yet."

"We'll drive into Molina tomorrow so you can get everything you need."

"Yes, great." He leant his elbows on the table and rubbed his chin with his clasped hands. "To be honest I'm rather glad that I'm moving now. Jenny is, er... well, something happened between us in the woods yesterday."

Come off it, I thought. "Really?" I said.

"Yes, I know it's strange, me being a bit old, but I knew she'd got rather attached to me," he said, reddening slightly.

"I know that, but you seem more like brother and sister, or uncle and niece."

"Yes, that's what I thought until yesterday. She came up to see me when I was painting, at about eleven."

"I didn't hear her leave the house."

He shrugged. "Anyway, she came and we sat down in the shade, chatting away as usual, then... then she took my hand."

"Right, well, there's nothing wrong with that, is there?"

He looked down at the table. "Then she said she was very fond of me. I laughed and told her that the feeling was mutual. Then she leant over and kissed me."

"What? I mean, how?"

"On the lips, a little kiss, then a bigger one."

"Did you kiss her back?"

"Well, yes, I am a man after all. You look shocked, Jack."

"I'm... surprised. I mean, you're a fine chap and all that but... what happened next?" I said, remembering Juanjo's horizontal embrace with Veronica.

"I held her away from me."

I tried to laugh. "You're joking?"

He shook his head. "I sort of wish I was, but I found that my mind had begun to work very quickly, for me anyway. I told her it wasn't a good idea for us to get involved in that way."

"What did she say?"

"She just smiled and nodded. She knew I was right really. She was embarrassed and began to get up, but I pulled her down and..."

"Ravished her?"

He frowned.

"Sorry."

"No, I thought it better to clear the air right away. I said that although I liked her a lot, I was a selfish man at heart and that I put my own happiness first."

"That was a strange thing to say."

He chuckled. "It just came out, but it's true. I pointed out that I'm twenty-five years older than her and she said that didn't bother her. No, I said, ten years from now I'll be an old man and you'll still be quite young. I told her I did hope to meet someone one day, but a bit nearer my own age, and that she should do the same."

"What did she say to that?" said the sprightly but still stunned thirty-nine-year-old.

"She said I might be right. She said she'd been impulsive but didn't regret it. I agreed, because I'd certainly enjoyed our kiss. We talked for a while and we both got over the embarrassment, then she left me to paint. Since then we've sort of ignored what happened and have managed to carry on as normal, but I think it's a good thing that I'm moving."

Just then I remembered the night when we'd almost bumped into each other on the landing. "Neil, that night when we went to tell her that we'd enjoyed her story, were you... just going to tell her that?"

He sighed. "Well, I must admit that I'd got into the habit of slipping into her room to say goodnight sometimes. I'd sit on the bed and we'd have one last chat, so I suppose you could say I'd been leading her on, though I didn't mean to."

I shook my head, still struggling to come to terms with this astonishing news, but strangely enough I felt only a little jealous. This bombshell blew my hopes out of the water, but I already felt relief creeping into my consciousness. I'd been fretting far too much, but about the wrong man, or had I?

"What's going on with that John Smith then?" I asked him.

"She's more or less decided to kick him into touch. She'll see him in London and tell him what's what, she says."

"More or less decided?"

He shrugged. "I hope so. He'll declare his undying love, she says, but she knows he's been messing around all summer, so she's determined to finish with him, and I'll be encouraging her, as he's no good for her."

"So do you think you and Jenny will be able to get back to where you were before... the kiss?"

"I don't see why not. It was only like having a snog at a party with someone when you're a youngster and then realising that it was just a drunken, impulsive thing."

"But you and Jenny weren't drunk, were you?"

He chuckled. "A little inebriated by the romantic setting, maybe. Oh well, one lives and learns."

He seemed relieved to have got this off his chest and at the same time quietly pleased with himself. It was as good a time as any to confess to my own seemingly hopeless aspirations, so I told him I'd been meaning to tell Jenny how fond of her I was.

He smiled. "I would wait a while, if I were you, Jack."

"Wait a while? No, no, that's it as far as I'm concerned. I was getting all stressed about her, but now we'll just remain friends. You've done me a favour really." He continued to smile. "Haven't you?"

"Jack, Jenny is, as they say, on the rebound, so take that kiss with a pinch of salt. She needs to go home and give John Smith his P45 before she'll be able to think straight."

"Do you think she'll come back?"

"Yes, I think she will, unless you frighten her away."

"Me? I'm not the bloody Don Juan around here, mate."

"Ha, very good, but seriously, you ought to relax more with her. She knows that you like her, and she likes you too, but now isn't the time to go beyond friendship."

I growled good-humouredly. "Says he."

"That was a mistake and she knows it; a mistake which I haven't told you about, all right?"

"All right. I'll get back now. See you there for lunch in a while."

"Yes, I'll do some unpacking. Which do you think will be the best room for an art studio?"

"One of the front-facing bedrooms. See you later."

"Yes, bye, Jack."

I went to the bar to kill some time and assimilate this weird new development. I'd thought of Jenny as being supremely self-confident, but realised that she had her weak spots like the rest of us. I called Paco down from his upstairs lair and immediately set about taking my mind off her.

"Paco, if Juan Carlos's family don't move away, do you think your son will be less likely to?"

"Edu? Oh, he's a stubborn one. He won't be influenced by what others do."

"I've only spoken to him twice, and not for long," I said, picturing the slimmer, more taciturn version of his father. "Why doesn't he come here much?"

"Because he doesn't like calling me Papá in front of others, and what else can he call me? He's an independent-minded man, but unfortunately the land ties us together."

"The land which he won't get until you die?"

"Ha, it's effectively his now, and I gave him the animals, as you know. No, if he leaves here he forfeits the land for the time being. I'll rent it out and we'll have a nice retirement. We'll go on cruises and blow all the money, or maybe I'll buy and restore a house or two." He raised his brows. "It's entirely up to him."

I stirred my coffee. "I bet he stays."

"Yes, I think he will in the end. There's a different atmosphere here this summer. Can you not feel it?"

"Well, last summer I was just passing through."

"That's true. Yes, there's something in the air. I'm sure we'll get someone new here by Christmas, and maybe someone else before next summer. Little by little we'll get this place back on its feet, eh?"

"I hope so."

"Will Jenny stay?"

"I hope so," I said without blushing.

"She's an asset. So lovely, so cheerful."

I pictured her kissing Neil. "Yes, she's great. Not really my type though. I'd rather find myself a nice Spanish woman."

"Yes, that would be good. Have you met Muñoz's daughter? The unmarried one who teaches in Tarancón, not so far from here?"

I remembered the pleasant, chubby woman of about thirty. "Yes, I've met her."

He grinned. "Well?"

"Maybe next summer I'll get to know her better. Bye for now, Paco."

27

Jenny and Neil's flirtation and my secret knowledge of it caused no perceptible change in our relationship, though Neil's move meant that we alternated our meals between his place and mine. Jenny booked a flight for the 2nd of October and the days ticked away pleasantly enough as the summer folk gradually left and the weather cooled.

On finishing the final draft of my book I emailed the document to Samantha. She called me three days later to say that it was a great piece of work and ought to consolidate my detective.

"Your readers will be crying out for more after this one, Jack. Do you think you can write another in a year, or is that not long enough?"

I smiled. "Oh, I think I can manage it, but let's say... fifteen months to be on the safe side."

"All right. Well, I'll send the book to the publisher's. I know they'll love it and we'll see what kind of cover suggestions they come up with."

I shrugged. "Yes, something similar to the last one, I guess."

"Of course. Who knows, ten years from now you might have a series of seven or eight books lined up on your shelf."

"That would be good," I said, thinking that twenty thousand sales of each one would be even better. With a little over a pound per book I'd do very nicely in Spanish Lapland, and my more literary efforts might make me a few quid too.

"I'll be in touch, Jack."

"Thanks, Samantha. Remember, email me first then I'll call you."

"Oh, it must be really wild where you're living. Ha, maybe your detective could go somewhere like that in your next book."

"I don't think so somehow. Speak soon."

"Bye, Jack."

As Jenny was still hard at work and Neil was busy painting pictures and doing minor jobs at the house, I resolved to get cracking on my deep, challenging, thought-provoking and highly original literary novel right away. There was no time like the present, I told myself, and although Jenny and I were getting on fine – better than ever, in fact – her presence made me restless. I'd have liked to have taken a trip somewhere, but with her departure drawing ever nearer it would hardly have been polite to do that, so I ripped the plastic off a new A4 pad, sharpened a couple of pencils and began to make notes.

I decided to set the novel in my home town of Hawick, beginning some years before the time of my childhood and ending more or less in the present day. I then wondered whether to make it a kind of family saga or a shorter, snappier affair, with paragraphs so profound that a lesser writer would need pages to convey the same information. Yes, a shortish existential kind of novel would be best, so that I wouldn't need to worry about word count at all. Like Oscar Wilde is rumoured to have said, I'd be able to spend all morning putting in a comma and all afternoon taking it out again, though on most days I'd probably do a bit more than that.

On the first morning I got this far and decided to knock off and arrange the shipment of my books, as I'd need them around me to get into a truly writerly frame of mind.

On the second morning I sketched out a couple of characters, before nipping round to Neil's, where I ended up helping him to stick down a few loose tiles in the bedrooms.

On the third morning I heard Jenny pottering about in the kitchen, so I went to have a quick chat. She made a pot of tea and the subject of her trip came up.

"In three days I'll be off."

"Yes, I know. We'll be sad to see you go."

"I don't think I'll be away for more than a month, all being well."

"Ah, yes, I expect you'll want to spend some time with your family, and see your friends."

She smiled. "That's right, plus the festival, of course. I think I'll take my rucksack and leave my suitcase here, if that's all right."

"Course it is," I said with a smile, as although the rucksack was big, the suitcase was bigger.

"Will you be able to drive me to Cuenca?"

"To Cuenca? No, no."

"Oh..."

"We'll drive you to the airport."

"Oh, there's no need to do that."

I shrugged. "It's only two hours," I lied. "And it's over an hour to Cuenca." I chuckled. "Anyway, when I go home I'll want ferrying to the airport too, as will Neil."

They were both insured for my car and Neil and I had more or less decided that we'd share it, as there was little point in him buying another one.

"All right, but when I come back I'll get myself to Cuenca, or even Beteta."

"No, you won't. You're not a mere lodger any more, but a good friend."

She blushed divinely. I then resisted a strong impulse to mention that Smith scoundrel and we chatted happily until Neil arrived for lunch. Every time the three of us met I observed them both for signs of secret yearnings, but I'd yet to detect any lovelight in their eyes, only friendship. Neil and I avoided discussing her departure and he seemed as philosophical about it as I was beginning to feel. Qué será será, as they hardly ever say here, and a few weeks without her would probably do me good.

On the fourth morning I shut my new notebook away in a drawer to give the six pages of random notes and diagrams time to ferment, I told myself, as I'd be able to concentrate much better once I was alone in the house.

Only one more thing of note occurred before J-Day, but it gave the three of us food for thought. We arrived at Neil's house for dinner on the eve of her departure and found him in a state of high excitement.

"What's up, Neil?" I said. "Has your new washing machine arrived already?"

"No, but come in, come in, it's something even more exciting than that."

It transpired that Encarna at the shop had told him that her friend had told her that a friend of Alfredo – the fortyish chap who lived in Albacete – was interested in coming to stay.

Jenny expressed mild enthusiasm, I was glad to see.

"What does he do?" I asked.

"I don't know, but Encarna's friend thinks he does things on the computer."

"Don't we all?"

"Yes, but if he can make a living doing whatever he does, it'll be great, won't it?"

"Did this friend of Encarna tell Encarna when the friend of Alfredo might be coming?" I asked, unsure whether or not to welcome this distraction so soon before Jenny's departure.

"In a few weeks, she thinks. She reckons he'll call Paco soon, so he'll tell us what's what," Neil said, before calming down enough to serve the spaghetti he'd made.

"If this person proves to be all right, who will he stay with?" Jenny asked a while later.

"With whoever's keenest to host him," I said dryly.

"Oh, I think I'll be up for it," said Neil.

"We'll see what he's like and which of us gets on with him best," I said, not wishing to overdo my drolly reticent posture.

"You won't give him my room, will you?" said the last person whose room I'd hand over to another.

"No." I willed myself not to blush. "This sauce is a bit spicy," I said, having failed. "Anyway, it's clear that the word is spreading about our lodger project, so if it isn't this chap it'll be someone else."

Neil nodded. "Yes, though the winter weather might put them off."

"Och," I said, a word I rarely utter. "It won't be half as bad as they make out. It snowed loads in Hawick when I was a kid."

"In Yorkshire too when I was a lad."

"I think I missed the real snow," said Jenny. "Though my parents swear it used to drift right up to the windows."

"Global warming," I said, and we talked about that for a while. I was relaxed and, I believe, rather witty, as by then I was almost sure that Jenny was going to come back.

I felt surer still when I carried her bag to the car, as it can't have weighed more than fifteen kilos. It took us almost three hours to get to Barajas Airport and although we'd been down to Cuenca a few times, the Madrid conurbation seemed horrendous to our unaccustomed eyes.

"It reminds me of the M25," Jenny said as we crawled along the last bit of the A-2. "And I won't miss that horrible road one bit."

An hour later we hugged and kissed her like a kid sister and set off back, Neil having taken the wheel.

"Ah, it'll seem strange her not being there when we get back," he said.

"That would be difficult. I don't mind her being away for a while. It'll give me chance to get down to some serious writing."

"And I'll get down to some serious work on the house, I suppose." He sighed. "It's going to be different now that all the summer folk have gone."

"You've got your painting."

"That's true, and I mean to take it seriously."

"And we've at least two months of good weather to come."

"Yes, milder and better for being out and about. So, have you decided what you're going to write yet?"

"I'm still planning it."

"Run it past me, if you like."

"I might. We'll see."

The following morning, after staring at my pad for a while, I realised that I wasn't yet ready to start plumbing the depths of my soul, so I walked round to Neil's to run something past him.

"Go ahead," he said when I'd outlined my idea.

After a cup of tea I went home, opened my laptop and began to write this.

Printed in Great Britain
by Amazon